Reboot Your Greek

Reboot Your Greek

A Forty-Day New Testament Greek Refresher

Darin H. Land

WIPF & STOCK · Eugene, Oregon

REBOOT YOUR GREEK
A Forty-Day New Testament Greek Refresher

Copyright © 2018 Darin H. Land. All rights reserved. Except for brief quotations in critical publications or reviews, no part of this book may be reproduced in any manner without prior written permission from the publisher. Write: Permissions, Wipf and Stock Publishers, 199 W. 8th Ave., Suite 3, Eugene, OR 97401.

Wipf & Stock
An Imprint of Wipf and Stock Publishers
199 W. 8th Ave., Suite 3
Eugene, OR 97401

www.wipfandstock.com

PAPERBACK ISBN: 978-1-5326-4831-1
HARDCOVER ISBN: 978-1-5326-4832-8
EBOOK ISBN: 978-1-5326-4833-5

Manufactured in the U.S.A.

For Jill

ἀγαπητή μου, προτρεπούσῃ καὶ φίλῃ

Contents

Preface | ix

Day 1: Dusting Off and Updating | 1
Day 2: A Great Tool, the *GNT Reader's Edition* | 5
Day 3: Alphabet and Pronunciation | 8
Day 4: (Re)building Your Vocabulary | 11
Day 5: Word Endings vs. Word Order | 14
Day 6: Noun Patterns | 17
Day 7: Review | 20
Day 8: The (Article) | 22
Day 9: Noun Patterns (Again) | 25
Day 10: No-Stress Prep(ositions) | 29
Day 11: Adjectives | 33
Day 12: Open-Faced Sandwich | 37
Day 13: Pronouns | 39
Day 14: Review | 43
Day 15: Greek Verb System (Overview) | 46
Day 16: Indicative Verbs (Overview) | 49
Day 17: Rapid Tense Identification | 54
Day 18: Common Tricky Verbs | 58
Day 19: Rapid Mood Identification | 62
Day 20: Finer Points of Tense | 65
Day 21: Review—Halfway Home! | 68

CONTENTS

Day 22: Finer Points of Mood | 70
Day 23: Help with Verb Identification | 73
Day 24: Little Words | 78
Day 25: Chunking for Success | 82
Day 26: To Be (Infinitives) | 85
Day 27: To Be Tricky | 87
Day 28: Review | 90
Day 29: Power! (Intro to Participles) | 92
Day 30: Level 1 Translation | 95
Day 31: Level 2 Translation | 97
Day 32: Level 3 Translation | 99
Day 33: Level 4 Translation | 103
Day 34: Level 2a Translation | 107
Day 35: Review | 110
Day 36: Genitive Absolute | 112
Day 37: So That's Why We Do It! (Periphrastic Construction) | 114
Day 38: Tools: Lexica and Parsing Guides | 116
Day 39: Tools: Bible Software | 120
Day 40: Review | 123
Day 41: Your Turn | 125

Glossary | 127
Appendix A: Quick Start Guide (Nouns) | 132
Appendix B: λύω Paradigm | 134
Appendix C: Participle Paradigm | 136
Appendix D: Participle Flowchart | 138

Preface

If you're reading this book, chances are you're one of the many people who have studied New Testament Greek in the past but have left it aside for just long enough that it feels very rusty. You're a little bit embarrassed to say that you *used* to be able to read the New Testament in the original language, but now the thought of trying to read a verse—let alone a whole passage—is scary. The very thought of it brings back bad memories of tests and quizzes in your Beginning Greek course in college or seminary.

You may sometimes think it would be nice to get back to where you were at the end of that course. However, the idea of slogging through that beginning Greek grammar all over again leaves you feeling overwhelmed. You may have even tried going through the grammar a time or two, only to give up, exhausted. Well, you are not alone. This seems to be a common situation. The causes are no doubt multiple, but the result is the same . . . a wish, a dream unfulfilled.

This book aims to give you credit for all that hard work you invested in your Beginning Greek course. I'm not going to ask you to redo that course as if you were coming to Greek for the first time. At the same time, I recognize that there are many things that you have forgotten. So what you need is a refresher. You don't need the whole course all over again, but you need to be reminded of all those things in a way that is manageable.

The first goal of this book is to get you back to where you were in a way that is relatively painless—as compared to your first go at Greek. The second goal of the book is to provide you with tools that may have been lacking from your first experience, tools which would have prevented the loss of your Greek in the first place. It would be little use to refresh your knowledge of Greek, only to see you lose it yet again. The fundamental idea of these tools is that the best way for you to retain your working knowledge of Greek is to read Greek regularly; and the best way for you to read Greek regularly is if the effort-reward ratio highly favors reward over effort.

This book operates on the basis of two bits of conventional wisdom to make the process manageable, on the one hand, and durable on the other. The first bit was given to me by one of my Greek professors (after I had had to relearn Greek myself, by the way). She claimed that it only takes fifteen minutes per day to maintain one's level in a language, while it takes thirty minutes per day to progress in a language. So the lessons in this book are geared to be completed within about thirty minutes per day. Well, actually, the *exercises* are so designed. It is not enough just to read the chapters; you must also do the exercises if you wish to get back to where you once were.

My working hypothesis is that you do not need to complete every exercise of every lesson. Spend thirty minutes or so on each exercise set and then quit for the day. Seriously! Don't feel that you have to master every aspect of every sentence of every exercise. Such an approach is likely to leave you feeling just like you did when you tried to reread your introductory Greek textbook—overwhelmed and ready to give up. Commit to spending thirty minutes per day, and I'm confident you will find yourself progressing at a rewarding pace. You will likely find that the things that are initially troubling will become clear as you progress through the book.

The second bit of conventional wisdom that shapes the form of this book is that it takes forty days of repeated action to form a habit. That's why this book has forty lessons. The hope is that you will complete one lesson every day for forty days, and thereby form a new Greek-reading habit. This new habit can be a lifelong habit of reading a little Greek every day. Consequently, you will never again find yourself in the position of being a former Greek reader.

There is a danger, though, in establishing a habit through the assistance of this book. It is the same danger that you faced at the end of your first-year Greek course—the habit of *not* reading

PREFACE

Greek, but doing a Greek lesson. There is a very real danger that you will come to the end of the lessons in this book and feel that you can relax, that you don't need to continue reading at the same pace. Perhaps that is partially true (my teacher said you only need fifteen minutes a day to maintain), but once you leave off reading—even for a day or two—the habit is broken and it is difficult to get that habit back. Think of your own experience! You know what it's like to leave off the Greek habit . . . and regret that later. I implore you, dear reader: determine now to make reading Greek—a little each day, and more some days—a lifelong habit!

One last piece of advice on this topic. Why don't you fortify yourself against the broken-habit danger described in the preceding paragraph? Instead of just doing the lessons each day, why don't you also commit to reading a New Testament passage of your choice for fifteen minutes every day throughout the duration of your forty-day study? That way, the habit you form will be truly a Greek reading habit, not based on the artificial crutch of a secondary book. And then when you get to the end of the forty days and feel like you need a reward break, you can reduce your time to just the fifteen minutes. It will feel like a well-deserved reward, but it won't come at the expense of breaking your good habit. Before you go on to the first lesson, decide *now* what investment you want to make toward your Greek reading future!

Day 1: Dusting Off and Updating

So, how long has it been since you read Greek? No judgment here, I'm just curious. Has it been one week, one month, one year, one decade? It doesn't really matter how long it's been, because memory is a funny thing. A lot of the stuff you learned is buried in there somewhere, but it's hard to find the key to unlock that memory. And losing the "key" can happen a lot faster than we might think. That's why I kept "one week" in the list. Even if you leave off your Greek reading for just a week, you can already begin to lose some of what you thought you would never forget. But don't despair! As I already said, a lot of that stuff is still in there somewhere.

Let me give you an example. When I was a child, I lived in the central African country of Burundi. I spoke some of the local language, Kirundi. In 2007, I returned for a visit after having been away from the country for nearly thirty years (aside from a brief visit about twenty years earlier). If you had asked me how to say, "Thank you," in Kirundi, I would have thought hard and then said, "I can't remember." But when someone gave me an ice-cold coke, I automatically said, "Urakodze chané" (phonetic spelling). That, of course, was the correct way to say, "Thank you very much." I didn't know I knew that, but the correct words came tumbling out of my mouth without me even thinking about it—words I hadn't spoken in at least twenty years!

Here on day 1 of your forty-day journey of rediscovery, don't be discouraged by how much you have forgotten. I'm going to try to help you find the key (or keys) to unlocking your memory of Greek, and, step-by-step, your recovery of Greek is bound to progress.

To that end, let's try the first key to see if it fits the lock. If you haven't already done so, pull out your old Greek New Testament. Blow off the dust, and open it up. What does it smell like? Like a new book? Like an old book? Does the smell bring back any good or bad memories?

Look at the words on the page you opened. Are any of the words familiar? Now try looking up a favorite verse by using the reference. (If you need to, look in the table of contents to help you remember the spelling of the NT book names.) Flip through the pages. What do you notice? Hopefully this process rekindles some of your excitement for reading the New Testament in the original language. It might also rekindle some of the fears you faced when you couldn't translate what your eyes were seeing. Push those fears aside and dwell in the excitement for a few moments.

By the way, which Greek NT are you holding? Perhaps it is the red-covered UBS edition, or maybe the blue-covered Nestle-Aland edition. Or maybe you're reading on a Kindle, smartphone, or other electronic text-reading device. These are all really great, and any of them will serve you well down the road.

But I want to strongly suggest that you purchase the United Bible Societies' *The Greek New Testament: A Reader's Edition* if you don't already have it.[1] Honestly, this tool is by far the best one known to me for helping people read the Greek New Testament on a regular basis. I feel so strongly about this that I would advise you to put this lesson aside until you have the *Reader's Edition* in your hands ...

... The *Reader's Edition* you are now holding is different from other Greek New Testaments. Instead of the usual apparatus (the listing of textual variants and other textual concerns at the bottom of each page), it has footnotes that provide English glosses for Greek words that occur fewer than thirty times in the

---

1. The United Bible Societies (UBS) have several editions of the Greek New Testament. Any edition will meet your needs for the present purpose, so long as you choose one that is a reader's edition—i.e., one that has an on-page or running dictionary with vocabulary entries at the bottom of each page.

DAY 1: DUSTING OFF AND UPDATING

New Testament.[2] This allows you to glance to the bottom of the page to catch the basic meaning of the words that you probably don't already know. Rather than having to suspend your reading for five or ten minutes each time you need to find a word in a lexicon, you can just glance at the bottom of the page, find a gloss for the word, and keep on reading. This greatly improves the speed with which you can read and therefore the enjoyment you receive from reading.[3]

By the time our forty-day journey is over, my hope is that you will be able to read much of the New Testament using your renewed understanding of Greek and tools like the *Reader's Edition Greek New Testament*. (You'll find discussions of other helpful tools on days 38 and 39.)

Exercise 1

Directions: Using the *Reader's Edition Greek New Testament* or another Greek New Testament, accomplish the following instructions:

1. Find the listing of the books of the New Testament according to their Greek titles.
2. Based on your knowledge of the English titles, try to sound out the names of each book in Greek.

---

2. A gloss is a one-word substitute for a word in another language. For example, *love* is an English gloss for the Greek word ἀγάπη. Of course, ἀγάπη has nuances and profundities that *love* does not have, and vice versa. So it is not proper to say that *love* is a definition (or even translation) of ἀγάπη. See the glossary at the end of this book for definitions of common terms such as *gloss* that will be helpful during your forty-day journey.

3. It is possible to use some electronic text resources to do much the same—except that they will give you a gloss for any word you happen to point at. This becomes a problem when you point to words that you should have known. Instead of activating your memory for words, you short-circuit the process of recall. You are less likely to progress very far in your facility with Greek. Nevertheless, if you stay alert to the possible pitfalls of using an electronic text, this can also be a viable option. See day 39 for additional information about electronic texts and Bible software.

3. Notice that the titles of each of the Gospels begins with the word Κατά. Do you remember what that word means?

4. Notice that each of the titles of the Pauline Epistles (plus Hebrews) begins with the word Πρός. Do you remember what that word means?

5. Using the page numbers from the table of contents, turn to each of the books in the text. Notice the titles at the top of each page. Depending on which text you use, you will probably see that the titles are in capital letters. Try to sound out the titles using these capital letters. Look back at the table of contents for the more common lowercase letters if you get confused.

6. Spend the rest of your allotted thirty minutes (see the preface) further re-familiarizing yourself with the format of your Greek New Testament.

Reminder: If you committed to spending an extra fifteen minutes per day, be sure to set aside time to do that today, too.

Day 2: A Great Tool, the *GNT Reader's Edition*

Yesterday I introduced you to the single best tool I know for helping to read Greek, namely, the *UBS Greek New Testament: A Reader's Edition*. As I mentioned yesterday, the *Reader's Edition* replaces the apparatus with footnotes. Each footnote gives the lexical form of the word to which it refers, together with a suggested gloss for that word. In addition, the following information is given depending on the part of speech:

Noun—genitive ending and gender

Adjective—feminine and neuter forms (if they exist)

Verb—full parsing

These bits of information, especially the gloss, save you many hours of stress and confusion in looking up words in a lexicon. Instead of flipping backward and forward through a lexicon to find the word you're looking for, a quick glance at the bottom of the page gives you the information you need. You can take a peek at the word, then keep right on going with your reading. No need to break the train of thought as you pause to wade through the secondary resources. And all you need to carry with you is the one Greek NT.

To take full advantage of this useful tool, it is helpful to keep a couple things in mind. First, the words included at the bottom of the page are words that occur less than thirty times in the NT. (It also includes verbs that are more common in terms of NT frequency, but tricky to parse—especially second aorists.) There's a good chance that you only learned words occurring fifty times or more in the NT during your first encounter with Greek. If that is the case for you, then there are a fair number of words that you will not have learned before that are not listed in the *Reader's Edition* footnotes.

There are a couple of options for how to approach this situation. One is to get a vocabulary builder tool (such as Bruce M. Metzger's *Lexical Aids for Students of New Testament Greek* or Robert E. Van Voorst's *Building Your New Testament Greek Vocabulary*) and learn the words in the gap. The second option is to use the appendix at the end of the *Reader's Edition*, which consists of a simple lexicon of the words that occur thirty times and more in the NT. Whenever you encounter a word that you don't know while reading, simply flip to the back of the text and look it up. The advantage of this method is that you don't have to memorize words. Instead, you will eventually learn the words through use. The third option is a variant of the second one. For this approach, rather than looking up unknown words, use the context of the word to help you learn the meaning by observation. Probably a combination of option 2 and option 3 will yield the best long-term results.

As with any book, the *Reader's Edition GNT* has some typographical errors, omissions, and other imperfections. Happily, there are very few of these kinds of problems in this edition. But when you encounter one, it can be frustrating. Most of the time when a footnote appears to be missing, the word was footnoted in a preceding verse on the same page. So when you think a word should be footnoted but isn't, before attempting one of the options mentioned above, try looking for the word in the previous verse or two. If you can't find it, then move on to option 2 or 3. If you try looking it up in the lexicon in the back and it's not there, that probably means it is an omission. In that case, you can either stick with option 3, look up the word in a full-sized lexicon, or look up your verse in a modern translation and try to figure out the meaning of your word by the process of elimination.

DAY 2: A GREAT TOOL, THE *GNT READER'S EDITION*

Exercise 2

Directions: Look up the following verses in the *UBS Greek New Testament Reader's Edition*.[1] Skim as many of the verses as possible in the allotted thirty minutes (see the preface). As you look at each verse, see if there are any words you recognize. Also, pay attention to the footnotes. See how helpful they can be! Don't worry too much about comprehension at this point. Celebrate those words you recognize (if any), but don't feel bad about the ones you can't figure out. We'll build comprehension throughout the coming forty days. (If you are able to read all the verses within thirty minutes, you may either read them again or read another passage of your choice.)

1. Luke 2:52
2. Mark 10:14
3. John 3:16
4. Rom 3:23
5. Rom 6:23
6. Eph 2:8–9
7. 1 John 4:7–8
8. John 11:35
9. John 8:12
10. Rom 1:16
11. 2 Cor 12:9
12. Eph 3:20–21
13. Rev 1:8
14. Rom 10:13
15. Gal 1:10

Reminder: If you committed to spending an extra fifteen minutes per day, be sure to set aside time to do that today, too.

---

1. If you have chosen to use an electronic text rather than the *Reader's Edition*, feel free to look up the same verses listed here. Practice looking up the meaning and parsing of words using the built-in tools.

Day 3: Alphabet and Pronunciation

Without looking, recite the letters of the Greek alphabet in order. How did you do? Were you surprised by how much you remembered, or by how much you forgot? No matter, it's good to review the alphabet as a way of getting back into Greek. Don't feel that you have to memorize the alphabet again. The main thing at this point is that you can read every letter and make the correct sounds associated with each one.[1]

Many of the letters look a lot like their English counterparts that are pronounced the same way, so we won't spend time on those.[2] Here are the ones you may have forgotten:

γ	gamma	makes the hard "g" sound (like gate)
		makes a "ng" sound when there are two gammas together (like singing)
ζ	zeta	makes a "z" or "dz" sound (like zoo or ads)
η	eta	makes a long "a" sound (like eight)
θ	theta	makes a soft "th" sound (like theater)
μ	mu	just like "m" in English

[1]. Recent research supports the claim that Koine Greek was pronounced more like modern Greek than like the "Seminary Greek" that you probably learned. Nevertheless, since this book aims to be a refresher for what you already learned—and since you probably already learned the "Seminary Greek" pronunciations—I will continue to use those here. If this topic interests you, you can learn more in Constantine R. Campbell, "Pronunciation," in *Advances in the Study of Greek: New Insights for Reading the New Testament* (Grand Rapids: Zondervan, 2015), 192–99.

[2]. Here is the complete alphabet: α, β, γ, δ, ε, ζ, η, θ, ι, κ, λ, μ, ν, ξ, ο, π, ρ, σ/ς, τ, υ φ, χ, ψ, ω.

DAY 3: ALPHABET AND PRONUNCIATION

ν	nu	looks like English "v" but sounds like English "n"
ξ	xi	makes the "ks" sound (like the x in taxi)
π	pi	just like "p" in English
ρ	rho	looks like English "p" but sounds like English "r"
σ	sigma	just like "s" in English (the sigma looks a lot like "s" when it comes at the end of a word)
φ	phi	just like English "f"
χ	chi	like the German "ch" (as in Lo*ch* Ness monster) or like English k
ψ	psi	makes "ps" sound (like oops)
ω	omega	makes long "o" sound (like no)

Hopefully the letters are coming back to you pretty well now. Let's move on to something just a little bit harder: doubled vowel sounds, aka diphthongs. When two vowels come together in Greek, they usually make a single sound—but not always. The trick is remembering what that single sound is and when they make two sounds. The rule is: If the two vowels make a diphthong, they make one sound; if they do not make a diphthong, they make two sounds. Here are the diphthongs you need to know:

αι	makes English "ai" sound (like the ai in aisle)
ει	like the Greek η and the long English "a" (like the ei in eight)
ευ	like "eu" in the word feud
οι	like the "oi" in oil
ου	like the Greek υ and the English "ou" (like through)
ᾳ, ῃ, ῳ	some people consider the iota subscript to be a diphthong; pronounce as if the iota isn't there—but pay attention to this letter later, as it makes a difference for translation

There's also the diaeresis, which is two dots over the second letter of what is normally a diphthong (¨), indicating that you

9

should pronounce both letters separately, like the "ai" in the English word naïve.

So, there you have it, a quick review of the things you need to know in order to read the Greek words out loud. We're not yet worried about knowing what all the words mean, just being able to sound them out. Understanding the words will follow along directly!

Exercise 3

Reread the verses from day 2's exercise. This time, read each verse *out loud*. Spend thirty minutes reading aloud. Again, if you are able to read all the verses within thirty minutes, you may either read them again or read another passage of your choice.

1. Luke 2:52
2. Mark 10:14
3. John 3:16
4. Rom 3:23
5. Rom 6:23
6. Eph 2:8–9
7. 1 John 4:7–8
8. John 11:35
9. John 8:12
10. Rom 1:16
11. 2 Cor 12:9
12. Eph 3:20–21
13. Rev 1:8
14. Rom 10:13
15. Gal 1:10

Bonus: Pick one or two of these verses and memorize them in Greek!

Reminder: Are you doing the fifteen extra minutes each day? If you didn't commit to that already, it's not too late. Start today!

Day 4: (Re)building Your Vocabulary

Building your Greek vocabulary is a complex undertaking. Second-language acquisition specialists tend to downplay the value of memorizing vocabulary words. Yet many beginners feel they cannot make any progress in reading the Greek NT until they have at least some basic glosses memorized. It is common for first-year Greek students to be required to memorize words that occur fifty times or more in the New Testament. But of course, unless you were an exceptional student, you didn't learn all those words with 100 percent recall the first time through. And yet you were able to read many of the sentences, exercises, or verses that you were assigned. You were able to do that by using contextual clues to help you remember the meaning of unknown words.

For these and other reasons, I do not recommend that you spend a lot of time re-memorizing long lists of Greek words and their glosses. Not only does that take a lot of time, it can result in discouragement as progress can seem slow—not to mention that it feels a little bit like punishment for not remembering these words from before.

On the other hand, without having a working knowledge of a critical mass of Greek words, you won't be able to even get started with reading a Greek sentence. You can't use contextual clues to help you translate an unknown word if all the other words in the context are also unknown!

So my recommendation for rebuilding your Greek vocabulary is twofold. First, simply read all the words in the dictionary at the back of the *Reader's Edition*.[1] The words you find there are

[1]. If you have chosen to use a Bible software program instead of the *Reader's Edition*, you can create your own list of vocabulary words by performing a word search for all words occurring more than thirty times, then having the

the ones that occur thirty times or more in the New Testament. Many of these words are the ones you would have been required to memorize for your beginning Greek course. This time, don't write out vocabulary cards, and don't memorize the words in the list. Just read the list several times over the next couple days. As you read, you will likely remember some of the words; others will seem to be foreign. No worries. Just aim to feel a little more comfortable with a few more words each time you read through the list.

Second, when reading from the *Reader's Edition* for the exercises or for your own bonus time, you will find that words fall into one of three categories: (1) words you already know, (2) words you don't know but are listed in the footnotes, and (3) words you don't know but are not listed in the footnotes. Words in the last category are likely common words (more than thirty times in the New Testament), even though you don't remember them now. These are the words you should look up in the dictionary at the back of the *Reader's Edition*. Again, don't memorize the word. Just note its definition and continue reading. Over time you should find that you have to look up fewer and fewer words in the dictionary.

Exercise 4

Open your *Reader's Edition* to John 16. Read as many verses as time allows from this chapter. As you read, do not worry too much about translating what you are reading, just try to recognize as many words as you can. Take a few moments to try to figure out each word before looking it up in the dictionary. But feel free to go to the dictionary as needed. If you can't quickly find the word in the dictionary, just go on to the next word. Finding words in the dictionary will become easier and easier as we review Greek morphology in the days ahead.[2]

---

program list the words and glosses. Check your software's help files for details on how to do this.

2. Morphology means the study of the various forms Greek words take to convey their function in a sentence. You can find definitions of this and many other important terms in the glossary at the end of this book.

DAY 4: (RE)BUILDING YOUR VOCABULARY

Reminder: If you committed to spending an extra fifteen minutes per day, be sure to set aside time to do that today, too.

Day 5: Word Endings vs. Word Order

Big Idea #1: Word endings, not word order, determine the function of words in a Greek sentence.

In English, it is clear who is doing the action of the sentence because the "doer" comes before the verb. For example, in the sentence, "Jesus loves the disciple," we know that Jesus is one who gives the love because the word "Jesus" comes before the verb "loves." You'll recall that the term for this is *subject*—"Jesus" is the subject of our sentence. Similarly, in this sentence "disciple" receives the love that Jesus gives because this word follows the verb. Because "disciple" follows the verb, "disciple" is the *object* of the sentence.

Greek follows a different model for encoding the subject and object of a sentence: distinct endings are added to the word to communicate whether it is the subject or object. The most common ending to indicate that a word is the subject of the sentence (or *clause*) is -ος. The -ον ending is the most common one to indicate that a word is the object.

To illustrate this, let us consider a made-up language, Greenglish. This made-up language uses English vocabulary with Greek word endings. The -os is added to the subject (like the Greek -ος) and the -on is added to the object and accompanying article (like the Greek -ον). The sentence used earlier becomes, "Jesusos loves theon discipleon." But there are several other ways to write this without changing the meaning:

> Jesusos theon discipleon loves.
> theon discipleon Jesusos loves.
> theon discipleon loves Jesusos.
> loves Jesusos theon discipleon.
> loves theon discipleon Jesusos.

DAY 5: WORD ENDINGS VS. WORD ORDER

All these Greenglish sentences are easily deciphered because we can easily see the -os and -on endings on the words. This allows us to easily transpose the subjects, verbs, and objects to their normal location in English. Translate this sentence from Greenglish into English: eats theon snakeon theos personos. Be careful here! You don't want the wrong creature getting eaten! The correct translation is, the person eats the snake. This sentence describes the time I ate python in Africa. Thankfully, I was not the meal that day!

There are two more common endings in Greenglish: -ou and -o. The -ou ending is used for possession, and the -o ending indicates the *indirect object* of the sentence. Add the English word "of" when translating the Greenglish -ou words, and add "to" when translating -o words. Translate this: theo childo theon bookon libraryou gave theos manos. In English this becomes: The man gave the book of the library to the child. Or: The man gave the library's book to the child.

Let's turn to Greek. The endings on Greek words are a little bit harder to recognize at first because they're placed on words you don't recognize. But once you begin to recognize the vocabulary, spotting the endings becomes easier and easier. Here are the endings you should work on recognizing at the moment—both in the singular and the plural:

	Singular	**Plural**
Nominative (≈subject)	-ος	-οι
Genitive (≈possessive)	-ου	-ων
Dative (≈indirect object)	-ῳ	-οις
Accusative (≈object)	-ον	-ους

Here are some simple Greek sentences and their English translations:

Original	Rearranged to English order	English
ὁ πατὴρ ἀγαπᾷ τὸν υἱὸν (John 3:35)	[no change]	The father loves the son.
ὁ δὲ θεὸς καὶ τὸν κύριον ἤγειρεν (1 Cor 6:14)	δὲ[1] ὁ θεὸς καὶ ἤγειρεν τὸν κύριον	But God also raised the Lord.
εἰς πάντας ἀνθρώπους ὁ θάνατος διῆλθεν[2] (Rom 5:12)	ὁ θάνατος διῆλθεν εἰς πάντας ἀνθρώπους	Death spread into all people.
τοῦτον τὸν Ἰησοῦν ἀνέστησεν ὁ θεός (Acts 2:32)	ὁ θεός ἀνέστησεν τοῦτον τὸν Ἰησοῦν	God raised up this Jesus.
ἠγάπησεν ὁ θεὸς τὸν κόσμον (John 3:16)	ὁ θεὸς ἠγάπησεν τὸν κόσμον	God loved the world.
ἔλαβεν οὖν τοὺς ἄρτους ὁ Ἰησοῦς (John 6:11)	ὁ Ἰησοῦς οὖν[3] ἔλαβεν τοὺς ἄρτους	Jesus, therefore, took the "breads"

Exercise 5

Directions: Reread John 16 from yesterday's exercises. This time, though, try to locate the subject and object of every sentence, as well as any possessives or indirect objects. Try to build up your understanding of each verse.

Reminder: If you committed to spending an extra fifteen minutes per day, be sure to set aside time to do that today, too.

1. Although it is true that Greek word order is very flexible, there are limits to the rearrangeability of some words. The word δέ, for example, always comes second in its clause. I have rearranged it to the first position here to follow English order, but it would never occur here in "real" Koine Greek. Otherwise, this sentence could have been written this way in Greek.

2. This is not a perfect example, because the word in the accusative, ἀνθρώπους, is the object of the preposition εἰς, not of the verb. But it does illustrate the point that word order is more flexible in Greek than in English.

3. Here is another word that normally comes second in its clause in Greek.

Day 6: Noun Patterns

Yesterday you looked at the most common noun pattern (remember, that's called a *declension*). You may recall that there are actually three basic noun declensions in NT Greek. The one from yesterday happens to be the second declension, but most textbooks take it first because it is the most common one.

Today we want to look at the rest of the noun patterns. I call this the Quick Start Guide for nouns (see appendix A). This guide is not intended to be comprehensive; it doesn't include every possible form of the Greek nouns. It does, however, cover the majority of noun endings.

Don't worry: you don't have to memorize the Quick Start Guide! It's designed to be a reference to hold onto and refer to as needed. (There is one tiny part of it, though, that I think you ought to commit to memory—more about that on day 8.)

Take a little time to familiarize yourself with the Quick Start Guide. You'll notice that the four main cases are there, listed in four rows: the nominative (row N), genitive (row G), dative, (row D) and accusative (row A). You'll also notice one singular and one plural column each for masculine (columns 1 and 4), feminine (columns 2 and 5), and neuter (columns 3 and 6).

As you look at the Quick Start Guide, see what patterns you can notice. For example, you might notice that every dative singular word (cells D1, D2, and D3) has an iota at the end—either as the very last letter, or as a subscript under the very last letter. You might also notice that most (but not all) accusative singular words (cells A1, A2, and A3) end in nu.

If your beginning grammar textbook was the one by William D. Mounce, you might be quick to recognize a couple other patterns in the Quick Start Guide. As Mounce helpfully points out, the nominative and accusative of neuter nouns are always the same as one another (i.e., cell N3 = cell A3, and N6 = A6). And the genitives and datives of the masculine and neuter match (i.e., endings in G1 = endings in G3, endings in D1 = endings in D3, endings in G4 = endings in G6, and endings in D4 = endings in D6).

Exercise 6

Continue studying the Quick Start Guide for several minutes. Mark it up however you wish to help you remember the patterns you see. You might use circles and lines to connect matching cells. Another idea would be to use different colored highlighting pens to point out the patterns.

Spend the remainder of your thirty minutes reading the following verses. I've given you more verses to read than I think you will be able to complete in thirty minutes. Don't try to race through them to check it off your list. Go for quality within the time limit, not for quantity.

1. 2 Thess 1:3–12
2. 1 Cor 1:18–25
3. Gal 3:5–9

As you read, use the Quick Start Guide to find the subjects (nominatives), direct objects (accusatives), possessives (genitives), and indirect objects (datives). As time permits, try to translate these verses. Check yourself using one of the more literal translations such as NASB or NRSV.

If you've committed to the additional fifteen minutes, perhaps you will want to reread the same passage you read yesterday. This time, though, try to use the Quick Start Guide to identify all the subjects and objects (based on the cases). In general, for your additional fifteen minutes, I recommend that you pick a book of the NT to read and read it all the way from beginning to end. Then pick another book and do the same. That is better than skipping around the NT for at least two reasons. First, it allows you to use

DAY 6: NOUN PATTERNS

context clues to help you understand what you are reading. Second, it gives you a goal (completing the book) that helps you stick to your commitment to read fifteen minutes every day.

This is the last time I'm going to remind you about your commitment to reading fifteen minutes "on your own" each day. Now you really are "on your own" on that!

Day 7: Review

Congratulations on making it through week 1! Now is a good time to look back at how far you've come in one week. I hope you are feeling more confident, as things are starting to come back to you with the help of the lessons, the exercises, and the use of the *Reader's Edition*. We've covered a lot of Greek ground this week, from the fine details (letters and sounds) to the big picture (word endings and word order), with a lot of stuff in between. Let's take time to review these things.

Alphabet and pronunciation. First, review the alphabet. Try reciting the letters in order without looking; then look back if you've forgotten any. (By the way, don't worry if you can't recite the alphabet. The idea is just to keep the letters fresh in your mind.)

Look back at the diphthongs—they're probably the most difficult part of remembering how to pronounce words in Greek. Remember that a diphthong is a pair of vowels that make a single sound, and therefore a single syllable. It's possible for two vowels to appear together in a word and *not* form a diphthong. In that case, the two vowels form two syllables, not one. This gets easier with practice. If in doubt, you can use Bible software to pronounce a word for you (more on Bible software later).

Word endings and word order. Here we touched on one of the most important parts of the Greek language. In Greek, the way that words are formed carries a lot more information than it does in English, while the order of the words carries less information. In English, we form sentences by placing the subject before the verb, and the object after the verb. That's how we know *who* is doing *what* to *whom*. Greek conveys that same information by changing the ending of the words. So the subject has one kind of ending (we call it nominative) and the object has another kind of ending

DAY 7: REVIEW

(called accusative). In addition to nominative and accusative, there are also genitive and dative endings. Remember that the primary function of the genitive is what we call possession, while that of the dative is for indirect object.

We used "Greenglish" to reintroduce the idea of word endings versus word order. Greenglish used an adaptation of the most common Greek noun pattern (second declension). Using the Quick Start Guide (day 6), we looked at the second declension patterns and other common noun patterns in Greek.

Exercise 7

Go back through exercises 1–6. Reread the verses and passages that you read before. Try to stretch for a little more understanding than you had the first time through. As time permits, read a few more of the suggested verses/passages from each exercise that you couldn't get to the first time through.

Day 8: The (Article)

I mentioned earlier that there was one tiny part of the Quick Start Guide that I recommend you memorize. That one part is the article (those twenty-four little words, all translated "the"). Here they are:

	Masculine	Feminine	Neuter
Nom Sg	ὁ	ἡ	τό
Gen Sg	τοῦ	τῆς	τοῦ
Dat Sg	τῷ	τῇ	τῷ
Acc Sg	τόν	τήν	τό
Nom Pl	οἱ	αἱ	τά
Gen Pl	τῶν	τῶν	τῶν
Dat Pl	τοῖς	ταῖς	τοῖς
Acc Pl	τούς	τάς	τά

Why are these twenty-four words so important that they warrant such attention? Because they will serve as lighthouses in the fog of Greek sentences. Sometimes you'll find yourself uncertain of this or that noun form. But when you locate the article, you can be confident about the case of that word because you definitely know the case of the attached article. Moreover, when you have a ready familiarity with the articles, you can more quickly identify the parts of the sentence. For example, if you know that τήν is the accusative feminine singular article, you will know immediately when

DAY 8: THE (ARTICLE)

you see it that you are looking at the direct object of the sentence.[1] The more familiar you are with the articles, the more easily you can make out which part of a Greek sentence is which.

I recommend that you memorize the Greek article by reciting the words out loud, moving across the rows (not down the columns). Why should you read across rather than down? Because reading across highlights the case of each form, whereas reading down highlights the gender. Although both case and gender are important, knowing the case is usually more helpful for understanding the meaning of a Greek sentence.

So, I urge you to memorize the Greek article extremely well. Memorize it so well that the words just roll off your tongue without giving much thought to it. This level of familiarity with the Greek article will pay great dividends in the long run. (Besides that, spending time memorizing is a concrete way of making visible—or should I say, "audible"—progress toward your goal of refreshing your knowledge of NT Greek. Some days ahead, you may feel like you haven't really learned anything going through all this. But at least you will be able to point to your memorization of the article as tangible progress.)

The article is the only thing in this book that I am asking you to memorize through "brute force." The rest is accomplished by simply reading and focusing reflectively on your reading.

Exercise 8

Read the articles out loud several times. Read across the rows, not down the columns. Write them out several times. Continue working on these until you can recite them out loud in under thirty seconds.

---

1. You may remember that there are other uses of the cases than the ones we discussed so far, so it is possible that this is not the direct object. Nevertheless, this only serves to strengthen the point—it is all the more useful to know the articles so that you can have great confidence in your identifications of the cases of words.

As time permits, read the following verses. Use the articles to quickly locate the subjects and objects in each verse.

1. Luke 3:21–25
2. Rev 20:7–10
3. Eph 3:8–13
4. 1 John 5:5–12

Day 9: Noun Patterns (Again)

Congratulations on your progress through this forty-day journey! Are things beginning to come back to you? After yesterday's focus on articles, plus the noun overview from a few days ago, you might be recognizing a lot of the noun endings that you encounter in your exercises and fifteen-minute bonus time. (You are keeping up with that fifteen-minute personal commitment, aren't you? Oh! I said I wasn't going to mention it again . . . oops!)

Well, it's now time to tackle one of the big mental hurdles of the refresher—the dreaded third declension. If you had a typical journey through your beginning Greek course, you were doing great for the first five to seven weeks. You had conquered the notion that case endings, not word placement, determined which word was the subject, which word was the object, and so forth. You had become fairly good at recognizing the case endings for common masculine, feminine, and neuter nouns. You were beginning to think that maybe all the horror stories about how hard Greek is were just not going to happen to you—but then third declension hit.

All of a sudden all those familiar endings started shifting on you. What used to be "for sure" a nominative, now just might be a genitive. And what your teacher had told you was always a genitive plural now shows up as a nominative singular! How can this be? Suddenly, panic began to set in, and you began to doubt you would ever be able to read Greek—real Greek.

If that scenario even remotely describes you, you may be feeling the third-declension panic rising within you again right now! You may have read the words "third declension" in the first paragraph and felt like giving up again. But if you have read this far, that means you have successfully fought off that first wave of panic! That's a step in the right direction, because you really can handle these things. You can do it, and I'm here to help!

Let me begin by saying that you do not have to completely master the third declension in order to enjoy reading New Testament Greek. You don't have to spend hours upon hours memorizing all the possible third-declension endings before you can begin to read the New Testament again. In fact, I estimate that you will be able to handle about 90 percent of third declension words if you simply remember the articles (which you've got down cold now) and the normal third declension endings. The last 10 percent you can get from context (usually) or by looking it up (only once in a blue moon). So you've already conquered the articles, and now let's look at that important "normal" third declension ending pattern.

But first, let me introduce you to a friend of mine. Her name is Sashia Es-own-sea-as. She likes to have her name repeated out loud over and over every time someone thinks of her! Sashia Es-own-sea-as . . . Sashia Es-own-sea-as . . . Sashia Es-own-sea-as.

Okay, okay, so you're thinking Sashia is my imaginary friend, but you're only half right. I didn't make her up (another Greek teacher did), but she's not imaginary; she lives in the third declension endings: S-ASH-I-A ES-OWN-SEA-AS stands for

Nom. Sing.	-ς	Nom. Pl.	-ες
Gen. Sing.	-ος	Gen. Pl.	-ων
Dat. Sing.	-ι	Dat. Pl.	-σι(ν)
Acc. Sing.	-α	Ac. Pl.	-ας

Once you are good friends with Sashia, it's pretty easy to recognize her aliases, er, I mean . . . it's pretty easy to remember the variants:

DAY 9: NOUN PATTERNS (AGAIN)

	Masc/Fem	Neut
Nom. Sing.	-ς/-	-
Gen. Sing.		-ος
Dat. Sing.		-ι
Acc. Sing.	-α/ν	-
Nom. Pl.	-ες	-α
Gen. Pl.		-ων
Dat. Pl.		-σι(ν)
Ac. Pl.	-ας	-α

Keeping Sashia Es-own-sea-as in mind, try naming the case of the following words. I've given the article to help out on most of them, since most of the time you'll have the article available in the New Testament, too! Cover up the case column and name each case. Then check yourself.

	Case	Number		Case	Number
ὁ αἰών	n	s	τῶν πατέρων	g	p
τῆς μητρός	g	s	τοῦ ἀμπελῶνος	g	s
ἄνδρες	n	p	τῇ ἀναστάσει	d	s
ὁ δράκων	n	s	ὁ ἀλέκτωρ	n	s
ἡ ἀνάστασις	n	s	αἰῶνας	a	p
τῇ ἐλπίδι	d	s	τοῖς σφραγῖσιν	d	p
τὰς νύκτας	a	p	τοῦ αἰῶνος	g	s
τῇ χειρί	d	s	πόδες	n	p
τοῖς ἄρχουσιν	d	p	τοῦ ἀστέρος	g	s
σώματα	n/a	p	τὴν σάρκα	a	s

How'd you do? About 90 percent? If so, you're right on track. If you really want to go deeper into the third declension, that's great. Here are the page numbers that cover third declension from several popular beginning Greek grammars: Machen 97–101, Mounce (2nd ed.) 75–88, Mounce (3rd ed.) 77–88, Summers (revised by Sawyer) 83–92. Feel free to look them up. But remember, you don't have to memorize all those third declension variants. After all, you're trying to read the New Testament in Greek, not write in Greek!

So, there you have it . . . a rough-and-tumble review of the third declension. Not so bad, right? Before I send you off to practice a little, let me say one more time: don't feel like you have to master the third declension before you move on to the next lesson. Don't get bogged down in the details. You'll pick up on the details as you practice more and more. Just concentrate on getting the basics presented here, and then move on. The last thing we want at this stage is to get discouraged. Don't even think about giving up now! You've tackled one of the rough spots head-on and you're coming out the other side. Be encouraged. You're making great progress!

Exercise 9

Read as many of the following verses as your time allows. Identify the third declension words and sort out the subjects, objects, indirect objects, and "possessives" in each sentence. Use one of the literal translations to check your work.

1. Rom 4:16–20 (Remember that the third declension -ος ending can lengthen to -ως.)
2. 1 Tim 1:17–20
3. 2 Thess 1:1–4
4. John 14:8–11

Day 10: No-Stress Prep(ositions)

Before we jump into some of the particulars of prepositions. Let me tell you a little secret: when you encounter a preposition in Greek, you can almost translate it into English with whichever English preposition makes the most sense in the context. So don't stress about prepositions. When you're doing your daily reading, just put in the English word that makes the most sense, and then keep on going.

But, of course, there's much more to prepositions than that. Whole volumes have been written on the use of single prepositions in Greek. And to be sure, when you are preparing for a sermon or an in-depth study of a passage, you will want to ignore the advice given in the preceding paragraph. But for now, just relax and recognize that there is a great deal of fluidity in the meaning of prepositions.

It may be helpful to take an example from another language. In Tagalog (from the Philippines), there are very few prepositions. In most places where we would use a specific preposition (such as in, on, near, by, under, over, etc.) in English, Tagalog speakers use just one word for all of these ideas. It makes for some interesting challenges in translation. Some Tagalog speakers struggle with which preposition to use when they speak English, because when they "think in Tagalog," they only have one general preposition in mind. Conversely, when a native English speaker listens to Tagalog, he or she can be confused as to which relationship is meant because the Tagalog preposition seems to lack precision.

The key to understanding the Tagalog preposition is to pay attention to contextual clues as to the exact relationship in mind.

The same is true in Greek (and, frankly, in English, too). Like Tagalog, Greek has fewer prepositions than English. So each Greek preposition has to cover more territory than an English preposition does—no one-to-one correspondence from the Greek to the English word! Greek handles this imprecision in the meaning of prepositions in one of two ways. First, like Tagalog, Greek relies on context to narrow down the sense intended by the preposition. These contextual clues are what make my "little secret" about prepositions possible. There are in the context of each Greek preposition contextual clues that the translator picks up on in order to select the correct English preposition. If, for example, the Greek sentence said something like *the person walked from the street, διά the house, and into the back yard*, you might correctly guess that the preposition διά means *through* in this sentence.

The second way that Greek handles the imprecision of its prepositions is by allowing the form of the prepositional object (not the form of the preposition itself) to narrow the meaning of the preposition. Obviously, we don't do that in English, so let's switch to Greenglish for an example. Let's say you wanted to say that the book is on the table. Easy in English, but in Greenglish there is no preposition, on. There's just one preposition, *epi*, and it can mean "on," "on the basis of," or "at." Since you want the reader to know which of those three meanings you intend, you say, *Theos bookos is epi the<u>on</u> table<u>on</u>*. If, instead, you said, *Theos bookos is epi the<u>ou</u> book<u>ou</u>*, that would mean the book is at the table. So, we can say that the case of the prepositional object determines the meaning of the preposition for many Greek prepositions.

There are a number of very common prepositions where this is important. Notice the handy mnemonic that often works for these: a gloss that has a prominent "a" goes with an object in the "a-is-for-accusative" case.

DAY 10: NO-STRESS PREP(OSITIONS)

Greek Preposition	Case of Object	Meaning or Gloss	Example
διά	Genitive	through	διά του λόγου means *through the word*
	Accusative	on account of [see the "a-is-for-accusative"?]	διά τον λογον means *on account of the word* (= because of the word)
ἐπί	Genitive	on	
	Dative	on the basis of	
	Accusative	at	
κατά	Genitive	against or down	
	Accusative	according to	
μετά	Genitive	with	
	Accusative	after	
παρά	Genitive	from or by	
	Dative	with	
	Accusative	beside	
περί	Genitive	concerning	
	Accusative	around	
πρός	Genitive	for	
	Dative	at	
	Accusative	to or toward	
ὑπέρ	Genitive	for	
	Accusative	beyond	
ὑπό	Genitive	by or from	
	Accusative	under	

Exercise 10

Translate as many of the following passages as time allows. Pay special attention to the prepositions and how they are used. Feel free to use this lesson's "little secret."

1. Rom 5:1–2
2. 2 Cor 6:3–10
3. Luke 24:5–7
4. Phil 1:3–7

Day 11: Adjectives

An adjective, as you recall, is a word that describes a noun. Beautiful, good, bad, and holy are common adjectives.

In English, there are three basic ways that adjectives are used, called attributive, predicative, and substantive. If I say, *the holy word goes out to all the earth*, holy is used attributively. Focusing on the adjective (*holy*) and the noun (*word*), notice that the two are bound together as a unit. The rest of the sentence says something about the unit.

Attributive	Predicative
Adjective/noun form a single unit	Adjective and noun separated by verb
Needs more to complete the sentence	Makes a complete sentence
Ex.: The *holy word* goes out to all the earth.	Ex.: The *word* is *holy*.

Notice how that is different from the predicative use. For example, *the word is holy*. In this case the adjective and the noun are separated by the verb (*is*), and a complete sentence is formed. The sentence is telling us the quality of the word.

The substantive use occurs when an adjective stands in the place of a noun, usually preceded by the article. Holy in the sentence, *The holy will see the Lord*, is an example of the substantive use. In this case we understand that the holy are the people who are holy; we could rewrite the sentence as *The holy people will see the Lord*.

Greek also has the same three basic uses of adjectives—but the way the attributive and predicative uses are formulated looks different from English. The key to distinguish between the various formulations is whether the article (any form of the Greek article, ὁ) is "on," or immediately before, the adjective. The article may or may not be "on" the noun. If the article is "on" the adjective, it is functioning attributively; if it is not, it is usually functioning predicatively.

Here are the most common formations:

Position	Example	Translation
1. Predicate	ἀγαθος ὁ λογος.	The word is good.
2. Predicate	ὁ λογος ἀγαθος.	The word is good.
3. Attributive	ὁ ἀγαθος λογος	The good word...
4. Attributive	ὁ ἀγαθος ὁ λογος	The good word...
5. Attributive	λογος ὁ ἀγαθος	The good word...
6. Ambiguous	λογος ἀγαθος	A word is good. *or* A good word...

Notice that ἀγαθος ὁ λόγος does not have the article (it's just before, or "on" the noun, λόγος, not "on" the adjective, ἀγαθος). In this example, therefore, ἀγαθος is in predicate position, and we translate, *the word is good*. Conversely, ὁ ἀγαθος λόγος does have the article (ὁ is "on" the adjective, not "on" the noun). In this example, ἀγαθος is in attributive position, and we translate, *the good word*.

Before we leave adjectives, there is one more very common use that we don't really have in English. We get close to it in the rarely used hyphenated adjectival form. Consider this sentence: *The around-the-world trip was too expensive for me to afford.* Notice how *The* and *trip* are separated by a hyphenated word phrase in the place where we would normally expect an adjective (such as The *long* trip). We could say that the article (the) opens a *slot* for an adjective, but in this case the slot is filled by a hyphenated phrase.

DAY 11: ADJECTIVES

In Greek, because it is fairly easy to see which article connects with which noun because they agree with one another in gender, number, and case, it is a lot more common for authors to put adjectival phrases into the adjective slot—no hyphens needed. Two of the especially common uses of this technique are (1) putting a prepositional phrase in the adjective slot and (2) putting a genitive noun phrase in the adjective slot. Here are examples of each:

	Greek	Hyphenated English	Common English
Prep. as adj.	Οἱ δοῦλοι, ὑπακούετε τοῖς κατὰ σάρκα κυρίοις (Eph 6:5)	Slaves, be obedient to the according-to-the-flesh masters	"Slaves, be obedient to those who are your masters according to the flesh" (NASB)
Prep. as adj.	καὶ εὑρεθῶ ἐν αὐτῷ, μὴ ἔχων ἐμὴν δικαιοσύνην τὴν ἐκ νόμου[1] ἀλλὰ τὴν διὰ πίστεως Χριστοῦ,[2] τὴν ἐκ θεοῦ δικαιοσύνην ἐπὶ τῇ πίστει, (Phil 3:9)	And I might be found in him, not having my from-the-law righteousness, but the through-Christ's-faith [righteousness], the from-God righteousness on the basis of faith	And I might be found in him, not having my righteousness [that is] from the law, but the [righteousness that is] through Christ's faith, the righteousness [that is] from God
Gen. phrase as adj.	δωρεὰν τὸ τοῦ θεοῦ εὐαγγέλιον εὐηγγελισάμην ὑμῖν (2 Cor 11:7)	I "gospelled" the of-God gospel to you freely	I proclaimed the gospel of God to you freely
Gen. phrase as adj.	. . . ὁ κρυπτὸς τῆς καρδίας ἄνθρωπος . . . (1 Pet 3:4)	. . . the hidden of-the-heart person . . .	. . . the hidden person of the heart . . .

1. Notice how the noun δικαιοσύνην comes before the prepositional phrase, but it is clear that the prepositional phrase modifies the noun δικαιοσύνην because the article τὴν opens up an adjective slot for the noun. This is the form seen in number 5 of the preceding table.

2. Notice here that the article τὴν opens up an adjective slot that is filled by

Exercise 11

As you read the following passages, pay special attention to the adjectives. Determine how each is being used, and translate accordingly. Do not worry if you can't translate everything. There are still many lessons to cover, so there are a number of things in these passages that we haven't gone over yet.

1. Rev 8:2–4
2. Rom 12:17–21
3. Titus 2:11–14
4. 3 John 11–12

---

the prepositional phrase διὰ πίστεως Χριστοῦ, but the noun that it is modifying is only understood, not stated. If you think of the article and its noun as the two pieces of bread in a sandwich, and the adjective as the sandwich filling, then you've got an adjective sandwich. When the noun is missing, you've got an open-faced adjective sandwich! When translating into English, you've got to supply the second "piece of bread" from the gender of the article and from the context.

Day 12: Open-Faced Sandwich

Do you like sandwiches? Fresh artisan bread on top and bottom, piled high with gourmet fillings in between. Or perhaps an "open-faced" sandwich, just one piece of bread topped with all the goodies.

I sometimes like to think of Greek noun phrases as sandwiches. The regular "sandwich" has two pieces of "bread," with a "filling" of adjectives between the two pieces. The bottom piece of "bread" is the article, and the top piece is the noun. The article introduces the noun phrase and makes a slot for the sandwich filling (i.e., adjectives). Sometimes, of course, we get noun phrases without the adjective filling—just going straight from the article to the noun. Tasteless, but nutritious.

Other times, though, we get an open-faced sandwich. We get the article (bottom piece of bread) and one or more adjectives (the filling), but no noun (top piece of bread). We get these in English, too, but they are less frequent. Here's an example in English: *The punctual will be served sandwiches first.*

In addition to being more frequent in Greek, these constructions also carry more information in Greek. Remember that the articles (and adjectives) in Greek communicate, not just number, but also gender. In the English example above, we can assume plural for number and both male and female for gender, but in Greek there would generally be no question about either of these variables. Most often, these constructions will be masculine plural, with the understanding that masculine is used when males only are in view as well as when a mixed company is understood.

Now the bottom line is this: I recommend that you get into the habit of transforming open-faced Greek sandwiches into regular, closed-faced English sandwiches. The reason is that doing so helps to convey the gender and number information that is embedded in the Greek forms. So, if you see a masculine singular article used for the open-faced sandwich, add the word *person* to your translation (unless it is clear from the context that an inanimate object is in view, in which case you would add the word *thing*). If you see a feminine singular, add *woman* (again, unless an inanimate object is in view). To a neuter singular, add *thing*. Add *people*, *women*, and *things* to masculine plural, feminine plural, and neuter plural, respectively.

Before we leave the topic of sandwiches, it is worth recognizing that the Greek language allows for a lot of "culinary" creativity! Greek has many adjectives to serve as ingredients for their linguistic sandwiches. But the Greeks didn't limit their sandwich fillings just to adjectives. They loved to add other things to their sandwiches, taking it to the next level of deliciousness. They commonly used prepositional phrases where adjectives would normally go. And since participles are a special kind of adjective (more on these flavor bombs starting on day 29), they often come in both closed- and open-faced sandwiches.

Here's an example of a sandwich with a prepositional phrase in the adjective slot: Πάτερ ἡμῶν ὁ ἐν τοῖς οὐρανοῖς (Matt 6:9, Our in-the-heavens Father; usually translated with a relative clause in English: Our Father *who is* in the heavens). And here's one with a participle phrase in the same slot: ὁ ζητῶν εὑρίσκει (Matt 7:8, The seeking person finds; again, usually translated with a relative clause: The one who seeks finds).

Exercise 12

Read John 12:44–46, watching for the use of the articles, adjectives, and prepositional phrases. (Be careful with this one—full of participles. If you struggle, don't worry too much. We'll talk more about participles starting on day 29.)

Day 13: Pronouns

Personal Pronouns. For the most part, Greek personal pronouns are easy for English speakers because they function in much the same way. In fact, the English person personal pronouns are probably more like Greek than any other part of the English language. That's because they actually indicate their function in the sentence by changing their form, just like Greek nouns and pronouns. (The similarity goes even farther for the third person singular personal pronoun, which also changes form for gender [he, she, it]).

For example, in English, we say:

I hit the ball. (not *Me* hit the ball.)

The ball hit *me*. (not The ball hit *I*.)

Your study is going well. (not *You* study is going well.)

She enjoyed the dinner (not *Her* enjoyed the dinner.)

The boy talked to *him* (not The boy talked to *he*.)

Conceptually, therefore, the Greek pronouns are mostly very easy; it's just a matter of learning to recognize the forms of the Greek pronoun. Take a look at the "Quick Start Nouns" table in appendix A, especially the first column. That's where you can find the various Greek personal pronouns.

So far, so good... but now for the hard part. The third person personal pronoun has two functions that really have no correspondence in English. So, the same word can do one of three things:

It can be a personal *pronoun* (just like English),

It can function as an intensifying *adjective* ("*same*"), or

It can function as an identical *adjective* ("*-self*" or "*-selves*").

The trick is to recognize whether the Greek pronoun is agreeing with a noun in gender, number, and case. Once you see that a Greek pronoun (and it's always in the third person form) is agreeing with a noun, you know that it's functioning like an *adjective* (i.e., either intensifying or identical adjective) and not a pronoun.

Now remember that there are two positions for adjectives, predicate and attributive. The predicate position does not have the article on the adjective, while the attributive does. It's pretty similar here with the pronoun (again, always the third person pronoun, αὐτός, and its various forms). If the article is "on" the pronoun, the pronoun should be translated, *same*. If the article is "on" the noun instead of the pronoun, it should be translated as *-self* or *-selves*, with the appropriate pronoun filling the blank.

For example, ὁ αὐτὸς λόγος would be translated *the same word*. Notice, by the way, that it's pretty easy to remember which one should be translated with *same* and which one should be translated with *-self* when you try to translate the Greek word-for-word into English. You can say *the same word*, but you can't say *the itself word*.

For *-self* or *-selves* examples, examine the following:

αὐτὸς ὁ λόγος *the word itself*

ἡ πίστις αὐτή *the faith itself*

αὐτου τοῦ ἄνθρωπου *of the person himself*

αὐταὶ αἱ γυναικες *the women themselves*

One more reminder before we're done with these tricky pronoun uses. There's a special case of *-self/-selves* usage. It happens when the third person pronoun is used as what looks like the subject, when in fact the verb form shows that a first or second person subject is in view. In such cases, we add the *-self* or *-selves* to the first or second person. Here's an example:

αὐτοι ἀγαπωμεν ἀλληλων. *We ourselves love one another.*

Relative Pronouns. The good news for relative pronouns is that they function in Greek very much the same way as English relative

DAY 13: PRONOUNS

pronouns. (Remember that the relative pronouns in English are who/whom or that/which.) The bad news is that, like adjectives, there are twenty-four forms of the Greek relative pronoun. Some of the twenty-four forms are easy to confuse with the various forms of the Greek article. The main key to spotting relative pronouns is that they have both a rough breathing mark and an accent; whereas the article (almost always) has one or the other but not both. Unlike the article, none of the forms of the relative pronoun begins with *tau*. Take a moment now to study the paradigm for the relative pronoun:

	Masculine	Feminine	Neuter
Nom. Sg.	ὅς	ἥ	ὅ
Gen. Sg.	οὗ	ἧς	οὗ
Dat. Sg.	ᾧ	ᾗ	ᾧ
Acc. Sg.	ὅν	ἥν	ὅ
Nom. Pl.	οἵ	αἵ	ἅ
Gen. Pl.	ὧν	ὧν	ὧν
Dat. Pl.	οἷς	αἷς	οἷς
Acc. Pl.	οὕς	ἅς	ἅ

As always, briefly study the patterns, but there's no need to memorize the whole paradigm.

A quick word about the use of relative pronouns should suffice. Relative pronouns introduce relative clauses. A clause is a part of a sentence that has a subject and verb (and sometimes an object and other parts). A *relative* clause, therefore, has subject and verb. Very often, the relative pronoun is the subject, but not always. The thing that makes it a relative clause is that it cannot stand alone as a complete sentence. Here is an example of an English sentence with a relative clause: He ate twenty ounces of lasagna, which is his favorite pasta. *Which is his favorite pasta* is the relative clause, and it is introduced by the relative pronoun, which.

Here are a few Greek examples:

Ἰακὼβ δὲ ἐγέννησεν τὸν Ἰωσὴφ τὸν ἄνδρα Μαρίας, ἐξ **ἧς** ἐγεννήθη Ἰησοῦς ὁ λεγόμενος χριστός (Matt 1:16).

And Jacob begat Joseph, the husband of Mary, from **whom** Jesus, the one called Christ, was birthed.

ἰδοὺ ἀποστέλλω τὸν ἄγγελόν μου πρὸ προσώπου σου, **ὃς** κατασκευάσει τὴν ὁδόν σου (Mk 1:2).

Behold, I am sending my messenger before you, **who** will prepare your way.

Καὶ εἶδον τοὺς ἑπτὰ ἀγγέλους **οἳ** ἐνώπιον τοῦ θεοῦ ἑστήκασιν, καὶ ἐδόθησαν αὐτοῖς ἑπτὰ σάλπιγγες (Rev. 8:2).

And I saw the seven angels **who** stand before God, and seven trumpets were given to them.

... ἔρχεται ὥρα ἐν **ᾗ** πάντες οἱ ἐν τοῖς μνημείοις ἀκούσουσιν τῆς φωνῆς αὐτοῦ (John 5:28).

... an hour is coming in which all the in-the-tombs ones will hear his voice.

Exercise 13

Translate as many of the following verses as time allows.

1. 1 Cor 15:1–2
2. Rev 8:2
3. John 2:23
4. John 17:2–8

Day 14: Review

Over the past week, we've been focusing on the noun system. We started with the article, then drilled down into the noun declensions. We looked at prepositions, followed by adjectives and finally pronouns.

Article. Remember that on day 8 I asked you to memorize the twenty-four forms of the article (the word that means *the*). I did this for two reasons. First, once you know the twenty-four forms of the article, you can use them to guide you through many Greek sentences. Even if you don't recognize the case of a particular noun (and therefore aren't sure whether it is the subject, the object, or something else), if there is an article with it you can figure it out from the article. Second, the article follows the two main noun patterns. So if you know the article, you already know those two patterns (with one or two minor exceptions). How are you doing with the article? Try reciting the twenty-four forms again now. Practice it a few times until you can recite it again today as quickly as you could on day 8.

Third Declension. On day 9 we looked at the endings for the third noun pattern. Remember our friend Sashia—I mean ς-ος-ι-α? Her last name is ες-ων-σι-ας. Look back at that pattern for a refresher. It's a good idea to keep this mnemonic in mind, since it helps you get about 90 percent of these third declension nouns figured out. Remember, too, that knowing the article can help you get to about 95 percent or more on these.

Prepositions. On day 10 we looked at prepositions. The most important thing to remember about prepositions is that many of the common ones have a wide range of meanings, and that those meanings are often narrowed down, not by the preposition itself, but the form (i.e., case) of the object. Take a look back at the common ones mentioned at the end of the day 10 lesson.

Adjectives. Greek adjectives are a lot like English adjectives. The central function of adjectives (both Greek and English) is to give a little more information (i.e., "modify") a noun. But how this is accomplished is a little tricky in Greek. First of all, a Greek adjective must match its noun in gender, number, and case (otherwise, you don't know which noun the adjective goes with). Greek adjectives, therefore, must have multiple forms in order to match all the possible combinations Greek nouns can take. To be precise, every Greek adjective must come in twenty-four forms (3 genders, 2 numbers, and 4 cases; 3 x 2 x 4 = 24 forms).

We also talked about attributive, predicative, and substantive uses of adjectives. In general, for attributive and substantive uses, the article is "on" the adjective; for predicative the article is *not* "on" the adjective. Look back at the charts in the day 11 lesson to review the syntax of these uses. Also, review the day 12 lesson, where we looked at what I like to call open-faced adjective sandwiches. This represents one of the common ways in which Greek noun phrases are constructed.

Pronouns. This week we also tackled pronouns (words that take the place of nouns). We explored personal pronouns (e.g., I, my, me, you, your, he, she, it, his, her, its in English, and αὐτός, αὐτή, αὐτό in Greek). We saw that Greek personal pronouns can act the same way as English personal pronouns, but they can also act in such a way as to call for a translation of *same* or *-self* or *-selves*.

In addition to personal pronouns, we also discussed relative pronouns. The syntax of relative pronouns is pretty straightforward, since they function pretty much the same way in both English and Greek. On the other hand, the morphology can be a little bit tricky at first. Look back at the paradigm (day 13) one more time.

DAY 14: REVIEW

Exercise 14

Reread the passages from the last few exercises. Try to recapture your understanding of those passages that you achieved on the first reading, plus try to stretch your understanding a little bit more.

Look back at the first few exercises, as well (day 1, 2, etc.). Consider how far you've progressed since you first picked up this book!

Day 15: Greek Verb System (Overview)

The Greek verb system is very robust. There are lots of variables, and with those variables comes a lot of power to express thoughts in refined ways. Complexity equals power.

Because I am a visual learner, I like to lay things out visually. Here is a visual overview of the Greek verb system:

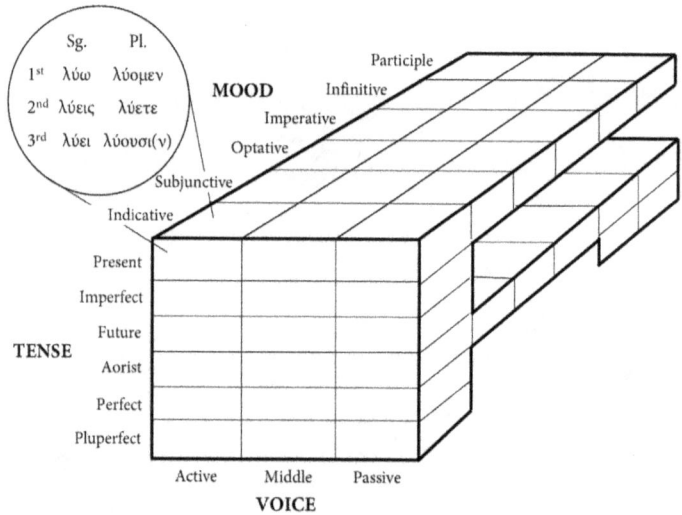

Overview of the Greek Verb System

In the days ahead, I would encourage you to look back at this visual overview frequently. It can help you get your grounding and remember how things work with the verb system. Let me point out a few details to get you started with your study.

DAY 15: GREEK VERB SYSTEM (OVERVIEW)

First, notice that it is a three-dimensional chart. That's because there are three main variables with the Greek verb system (one for each axis of the chart): tense, voice, and mood. You will probably remember those terms from your previous study, so a quick reminder will suffice here.

There are six tenses: present, imperfect, future, aorist, perfect, and pluperfect. We'll go into more detail on these later, but for now, just focus on the basic idea of each. The present is for ongoing action, usually in the "now" time. The imperfect is for ongoing action in the past time. The future is for, well, future action. The perfect is for past action with consequences in the present, and the pluperfect is one step further back in time from the perfect (i.e., action before a specific time in the past, with consequence up to that specific time).

There are three voices: active, middle, and passive. The active means the subject does the action (e.g., the boy hit the ball); the passive means the subject receives the action (e.g., the boy was hit by the ball); and the middle—well, that's a little trickier, since we don't have that one in English. Basically, we can say that in the middle, the subject is somehow closely involved in the action, sometimes doing the action *for* (but not necessarily *to*) oneself.

There are six moods:

Indicative—for general statements and questions

Subjunctive—for possibilities, often translated with might, would, should, etc.

Optative—for wish (when used in positive statements) or strong prohibitions (when used in negative statements)

Imperative—for commands or requests

Infinitive—verbal nouns ("*To err* is human, but *to forgive* is divine.")

Participle—verbal adjectives ("Let *sleeping* dogs lie.")

The second feature of the chart that you should notice is that most of the "boxes" in the chart have more than one element, or word, inside. That's because there are more variables than the three main ones. The reason that I didn't try to capture all the variables at once is that (a) we live in a three-dimensional world, so trying to make a six- or seven-dimensional chart would be impossible to visualize. And (b), the variables are different for the different "boxes," depending on which mood we're looking at. I've only expanded one of the boxes to illustrate that there are six words in that box. But all the other boxes (except infinitives) could likewise be expanded.

In each box in the indicative mood, there are two more variables: person (1st, 2nd, or 3rd) and number (singular or plural). The same is true for the subjunctive and optative moods. The imperative mood is similar, but it only has second and third person, not first person. (Compare English imperative, which only has second person.) The infinitive has only one form per box, so that's pretty simple—and surprising. With all the power in the other forms of the Greek language system, one would expect the infinitive to be more complex. (Actually, there is some complexity in the Greek infinitive, but it comes at the syntax level, not the morphology level.)

Finally, notice that only the present and aorist tenses exist in all of the moods. The perfect exists in a number of the moods, but the imperfect, future, and pluperfect exist only in the indicative. (Well, that's not entirely true: the future also exists in the participle, but it's so rare that I didn't include it on the chart.)

Exercise 15

Reread yesterday's passages, this time paying attention to the verbs. How many verbs can you spot? Can you guess what tense, voice, and mood each is? (If not, that's perfectly fine for now. We'll fill in more details in the days ahead.) Study the verbs in each of your translations; then look back to how those verbs are formed in Greek. Do you recognize any patterns? If time permits, look again at the verbs in the passages from exercise 9 with these same questions in mind.

Day 16: Indicative Verbs (Overview)

More than half of verbs in the New Testament are in the indicative mood (15,623 out of 28,110 total verb instances). The remaining instances are distributed among the other five moods. If for no other reason, this dominance alone suggests the importance of attending to the indicative mood. A second reason to pay special attention to the indicative mood, alluded to in yesterday's lesson, is that the indicative mood is the only one in which all the tenses occur. Gaining ease in recognizing the signs of the various tenses (tomorrow's topic) is best accomplished in the indicative mood.

Recall that the indicative mood is used to make statements and ask questions about the way things were, are, or will be; it is sometimes called the mood of communicated reality. Sentences like the following use verbs in the indicative mood:

- The piano emitted beautiful music.
- The painting enhances the ambiance of the room.
- The chair had been placed in the optimal position.

The six Greek tenses can usually be translated into English verbs according to the following rules of thumb. We'll return to this topic in a later lesson, but for now you can follow these rules:

Greek Tense	Greek Example	English Tense	English Translation
Present	Matt 3:11 Ἐγὼ μὲν ὑμᾶς **βαπτίζω** ἐν ὕδατι εἰς μετάνοιαν.	Present Progressive	On the one hand, I **am baptizing** you in water for repentance.
Imperfect	Luke 16:1 **Ἤκουον** δὲ ταῦτα πάντα οἱ Φαρισαῖοι.	Past Progressive	Now the Pharisees **were hearing** all these things.

Greek Tense	Greek Example	English Tense	English Translation
Future	John 5:25 οἱ νεκροὶ **ἀκούσουσιν** τῆς φωνῆς τοῦ υἱοῦ τοῦ θεοῦ.	Future	The dead **will hear** the voice of the Son of God.
Aorist	John 7:31 Ἐκ τοῦ ὄχλου δὲ πολλοὶ **ἐπίστευσαν** εἰς αὐτὸν	Simple Past	Now many from the crowd **believed** in him.
Perfect	Luke 10:19 ἰδοὺ **δέδωκα** ὑμῖν τὴν ἐξουσίαν τοῦ πατεῖν ἐπάνω ὄφεων καὶ σκορπίων, καὶ ἐπὶ πᾶσαν τὴν δύναμιν τοῦ ἐχθροῦ.	Perfect	Behold, I **have given** you the authority to tread upon serpents and scorpions, and over all the power of the enemy.
Pluperfect	John 11:57 **δεδώκεισαν** δὲ οἱ ἀρχιερεῖς καὶ οἱ Φαρισαῖοι ἐντολὰς.	Past Perfect	Now the chief priests and the Pharisees **had given** commands.

Take a few minutes to study the following table. Notice that the table only includes the third person singular verbs.

1. I have translated these middle forms using the idea of self-interest, which is one of the possible senses conveyed by the middle voice in Greek. Recall that the middle voice in New Testament Greek often functions much like the active voice, except with additional emphasis on the subject. Consult an intermediate or advanced grammar for additional information.

DAY 16: INDICATIVE VERBS (OVERVIEW)

	Active	Middle[1]	Passive
Present • Ongoing or simple • Dictionary form	πιστεύει he/she/it is believing βλέπει he/she/it is seeing ἀκούει he/she/it is hearing γεννᾷ[2] he/she/it is giving birth	πιστεύεται he/she/it is believing for himself/herself/itself βλέπεται he/she/it is seeing for himself/herself/itself ἀκούεται he/she/it is hearing for himself/herself/itself γεννᾶται he/she/it is giving birth for himself/herself/itself	πιστεύεται he/she/it is being believed βλέπεται he/she/it is being seen ἀκούεται he/she/it is being heard γεννᾶται he/she/it is being given birth
Future • Like Present, except with σ (or sometimes ψ or ξ) toward end	πιστεύσει he/she/it will believe βλέψει he/she/it will see ἀκούσει he/she/it will hear γεννήσει he/she/it will give birth	πιστεύσεται he/she/it will believe for himself/herself/itself βλέψεται he/she/it will see for himself/herself/itself ἀκούσεται he/she/it will hear for himself/herself/itself γεννήσεται he/she/it will give birth for himself/herself/itself	πιστευθήσεται he/she/it will be believed βλεφθήσεται he/she/it will be seen ἀκουσθήσεται he/she/it will be heard γεννηθήσεται he/she/it will be given birth

2. The lexical form of this word is γεννάω. Verbs whose lexical forms end in -αω, -εω, or -οω are called contract verbs. The α, ε, or ο (i.e., the "contract

REBOOT YOUR GREEK

	Active	Middle	Passive
Aorist • Usually simple past • ἐ or lengthened vowel at beginning • Usually with σ (or sometimes ψ or ξ) toward end	ἐπίστευσε(ν) he/she/it believed	ἐπιστεύσατο he/she/it believed for himself/herself/itself	ἐπιστεύθη he/she/it was believed
	ἔβλεψε(ν) he/she/it saw	ἐβλέψατο he/she/it saw for himself/herself/itself	ἐβλέφθη he/she/it was seen
	ἤκουσε(ν) he/she/it heard	ἠκούσατο he/she/it heard for himself/herself/itself	ἠκούσθη he/she/it was heard
	ἐγέννησεν he/she/it gave birth	ἐγεννήσατο he/she/it gave birth for himself/herself/itself	ἐγεννήθη he/she/it was given birth
Imperfect • Continuous or repeated past • ἐ or lengthened vowel at beginning • No σ	ἐπίστευε(ν) he/she/it was believing	ἐπιστεύετο he/she/it was believing for himself/herself/itself	ἐπιστεύετο he/she/it was being believed
	ἔβλεπε(ν) he/she/it was seeing	ἐβλέπετο he/she/it was seeing for himself/herself/itself	ἐβλέπετο he/she/it was being seen
	ἤκουε(ν) he/she/it was hearing	ἠκούετο he/she/it was hearing for himself/herself/itself	ἠκούετο he/she/it was being heard
	ἐγέννα he/she/it was giving birth	ἐγεννᾶτο he/she/it was giving birth for himself/herself/itself	ἐγεννᾶτο he/she/it was being given birth

---

vowels") contract with the connecting vowel and verb ending, and the contraction is marked with a circumflex. In tenses that use tense formatives, the α, ε, or ο lengthen.

DAY 16: INDICATIVE VERBS (OVERVIEW)

	Active	Middle	Passive
Perfect	πεπιστευκε(ν)	πεπίστευται	πεπίστευται
• Past event with present consequences	he/she/it has believed	he/she/it has believed for himself/herself/itself	he/she/it has been believed
• Usually repeated first consonant	—³ he/she/it has seen	— he/she/it has seen for himself/herself/itself	— he/she/it has been seen
• Usually with κ toward end in Active	—⁴ he/she/it has heard	— he/she/it has heard for himself/herself/itself	— he/she/it has been heard
	γεγέννηκε(ν) he/she/it has given birth	γεγέννηται he/she/it has given birth for himself/herself/itself	γεγέννηται he/she/it has been given birth

Exercise 16

Translate as many of these passages as time allows. Pay attention to the tenses of the indicative verbs.

1. Matt 7:24
2. Matt 13:34
3. John 7:31
4. John 16:6
5. Acts 18:8

---

3. βλέπω does not occur in the perfect tense in the New Testament.

4. I have not included the perfect of ἀκούω in this chart because its form is irregular. The perfect of ἀκούω is ἀκήκοα.

Day 17: Rapid Tense Identification

Identifying the tense of a verb can be a little bit tricky, especially for beginners. Even for those who have been reading Greek for a long time, some of the trickier verbs can cause confusion. But getting the tense right is really important!

There is good news, though. A few key signs make identifying the tense a lot easier in the vast majority of instances. It does take some practice, and beginners often miss the key signs because the details of voice and mood, as well as person and number, distract them. The crucial thing here is to get the signs firmly in your mind—don't lose track of these keys. I sometimes see students who can recite the signs of the tenses, but they forget to think about them when they actually try to determine the tense of verbs. Don't let that happen to you! At the end of this lesson, I'll give you a little flowchart to walk you through the decision-making process in determining the tense. You may not need the flowchart, but it may be useful just to remind you to go through the thought process.

Before we get to that flowchart, let's jump right into the common signs of the tenses.

Tense	Sign	Example	Expanded
Future	no augment,[1] sigma	λύσω	(λυ-σ-ω)
1st Aorist	augment, sigma	ἔλυσα	(ε-λυ-σ-α)
2nd Aorist	augment, stem-change	ἔλαβον	(ε-λαβ-ον)

1. Remember that an augment is usually an epsilon added to the beginning of a word (e.g., ποιέω → ἐποίει). It could also be a lengthened vowel at the beginning of a word that already begins with a vowel.

DAY 17: RAPID TENSE IDENTIFICATION

Tense	Sign	Example	Expanded
Aor. Passive	augment, theta-eta	ἐλύθην	(ε-λυ-θη-α)
Imperfect	augment, no sigma/no stem-change	ἔλυον	(ε-λυ-ον)
Perfect	reduplication,[2] kappa	λέλυκα	(λε-λυ-κ-α)
Pluperfect	opt. augment, reduplication, κει	ἐλελύκειν	(ε-λε-λυ-κει-ν)
Present	none of the above; lexical form	λύω	(λυ-ω)

Not every instance of every verb displays these signs, but most of the time, these signs will be there. And when you see these signs, you can pretty much count on them.

Now, a few words by way of reminder regarding how to identify these signs in practice. For starters, remember that the augments and reduplications normally come at the very beginning of the verb. But if the verb is compounded—usually by the addition of a prepositional prefix—the augment or reduplication comes between the prefix and the main part of the verb. (For example, λαμβάνω becomes ἔλαβεν in the aorist, while προλαμβάνω becomes προέλαβεν. Notice the epsilon augment coming before the λαβ in both aorist forms.) And if the verb begins with a vowel, the reduplication or augment can take the form of a lengthening of that initial vowel. (For example, the aorist of ἀγαπάω is ἠγάπησα. Notice the augment in the form of an alpha lengthened to eta.)

Also remember that all the letter signs (the sigmas for future and aorist, the theta-eta for aorist passive, and the kappa for perfect and reduplication) occur after the stem but before the personal endings. This can get tricky if you aren't real familiar with the verb stems and the personal endings. But don't get too stressed about stems and endings. There are many tools that can help you identify the tense, especially for the harder ones (more on this in a later lesson). Keep

---

2. Remember that reduplication is usually the first consonant of a word added again to the beginning of the word and connected with an epsilon (e.g., ποιέω → πεποίηκεν). It could also take the form of a lengthened vowel at the beginning of a word that already begins with a vowel (yes, just like the augment).

in mind that tense identification definitely gets easier with practice. Don't be discouraged if you make mistakes now and then.

Some people find it really helpful to memorize the principle parts of the common verbs. I'm not going to advocate that strongly; however, I can say that doing so has two potential benefits: (1) it gives you confidence in identifying the memorized verbs and (2) it helps the patterns of the tenses get ingrained in your subconscious for easier recall identifying the tenses of other verbs. The appendices in standard Beginning Greek textbooks often have lists of the principle parts of common verbs in the appendices (pp. 385–95 in Mounce 2nd ed.; pp. 372–80 in Mounce 3rd ed.).

Here is the simple flowchart promised earlier:

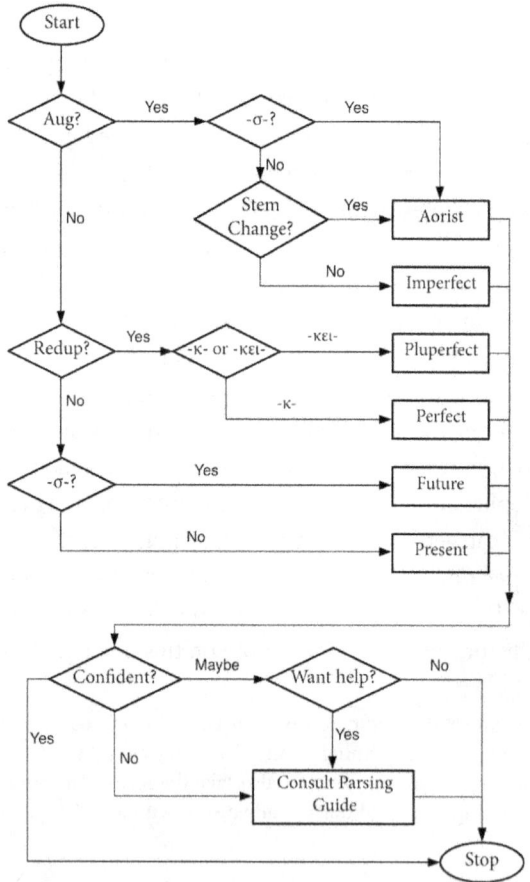

DAY 17: RAPID TENSE IDENTIFICATION

Rapid Tense Identification of Indicative Verbs

Exercise 17

Make your way through John 4, beginning at v. 4. As always, keep at it until your time limit is reached. Go for quality, not quantity. As you read, pay special attention to the verbs. Try to identify the tense, voice, and mood of each verb as much as possible.

Day 18: Common Tricky Verbs

In yesterday's lesson, I mentioned first and second aorist. You will remember from your past study that the distinction between the first and second aorist is one of form, not function. So, it's a matter of recognizing the tense, and then the translation follows. In other words, no matter how a word looks, if it is an aorist it still gets translated as an aorist (i.e., with the English simple past for basic translation of the aorist in the indicative mood).

Generally speaking, the first aorist is the easier one to spot: it's got the augment and the sigma. The second aorist is harder because it could look just like the imperfect; both have the augment but no sigma. The difference is that the second aorist has a stem that is different from the present stem (or the lexical form). Sometimes the change is radical (as in τρέχω, with imperfect form ἔτρεχον and aorist form ἔδραμον), and sometimes the change is very subtle (as in γίνομαι, with imperfect form ἐγινόμην and aorist form ἐγενόμην). The good news, though, is that most second aorists are very common, and the list of common second aorists is short. Here are the ones that you should become familiar with. (The ones marked with an arrow are compounded forms of the previous word.)

Lexical Form	2nd Aorist Form	Aorist Gloss
ἄγω	ἤγαγον	I brought, led
→ συνάγω	συνήγαγον	I gathered
ἀποθνήσκω	ἀπέθανον	I died
ἀπόλλυμι	ἀπώλεσα	I destroyed

DAY 18: COMMON TRICKY VERBS

Lexical Form	2nd Aorist Form	Aorist Gloss
βαίνω	βήν[1]	I went
→ ἀναβαίνω	ἀνέβην	I went up
→ καταβαίνω	κατέβην	I went down
βάλλω	βάλω	I threw
→ ἐκβάλλω	βάλω	I threw out
γίνομαι	ἐγενόμην	I became
γινώσκω	ἔγνων	I knew
ἔρχομαι	ἦλθον	I came
→ ἀπέρχομαι	ἀπῆλθον	I departed
→ εἰσέρχομαι	εἰσῆλθον	I entered
→ ἐξέρχομαι	ἐξῆλθον	I exited
→ προσέρχομαι	προσῆλθον	I approached
ἐσθίω	ἔφαγον	I ate
εὑρίσκω	εὗρον	I found
ἔχω	ἔσχον	I had
λαμβάνω	ἔλαβον	I received, I took
λέγω	εἶπον	I said
ὁράω	εἶδον	I saw
πίνω	ἔπιον	I drank
πίπτω	ἔπεσα	I fell

Remember, there is no need to memorize this list; just keep the list handy while reading until you remember them. Moreover, if you're using the *Greek NT Reader's Edition*, these aorist forms are noted in the footnotes, even though they're common.

1. This exact form does not appear in the NT, but it does appear in compounded forms.

Another category of tricky verbs is the -μι verbs. Remember that the -μι verbs take a slightly different set of endings from the more common -ω verbs. Here are the primary endings:

	ω conjugation	μι conjugation
1 sg	-ω	-μι
2 sg	-εις	-ς
3 sg	-ει	-σιν
1 pl	-μεν	-μεν
2 pl	-τε	-τε
3 pl	-ουσι(ν)	-ασιν

Remember, too, that -μι verbs have ι-reduplication in the present (same as regular reduplication, except that the repeated consonant is connected to the stem with an ι instead of with an ε). And also remember that -μι verbs usually have κ as the tense formative in the aorist instead of the σ tense formative found in the -ω conjugation. This can lead the unwary reader to mistake an aorist of a -μι verb for a perfect. Attention to the presence of reduplication (for perfect) or absence of reduplication (for aorist) is the key here.

Like the second aorists, there aren't too many -μι verbs, and most are fairly common. The ones that you should pay the most attention to are δίδωμι and ἵστημι (and the various compounded forms of ἵστημι). δίδωμι is actually fairly straight forward; ἵστημι is the one that can get hard to identify. I sometimes say that if you come across a verb that you can't seem to track down and identify—and if it has a στ in it somewhere—try ἵστημι.

One bit of good news here with the -μι verbs and the second aorists. Many of the tools that we will be covering in a later lesson have extra help for these. So, the advice remains: familiarization not memorization. Use the tools when you get stuck.

There's one more verb that deserves mention in this lesson: οἶδα. οἶδα is a perfect form with a present meaning. (The pluperfect form carries the aorist meaning.) Your tools will often parse

DAY 18: COMMON TRICKY VERBS

the verb according to its form, leaving you to translate with the appropriate meaning.

Exercise 18

Read Matthew 28, beginning in v. 8. As always, read as many verses as you can read with understanding in your thirty minutes. Pay special attention to the formation and usage of second aorist verbs. Also note any -μι verbs you come across.

Day 19: Rapid Mood Identification

A few days ago, we looked at rapid tense identification. Aside from recognizing the person and number of a verb, tense identification is perhaps the most important skill for reading with a high degree of fluidity. (Of course, recognizing the lexical form of the word so as to be able to know the semantic meaning of the word is indispensable, too.)

Next in importance is identifying the mood of a verb. In this lesson, I will give you a few tips for rapidly identifying the mood. As with many of the tips discussed so far, these guidelines will not permit you to identify the mood of 100 percent of the verb forms in the New Testament. However, they will help you to identify the vast majority of them, thus allowing you to read the New Testament with greater ease.

The mood of the remaining verb forms is often identified in the secondary resources to be discussed in a later lesson. For now, let's focus on the signs of the non-indicative moods that are most readily identifiable. Before we get started, I invite you to look back at the overview of the entire Greek verb system as presented on day 10. That will help you get your bearings as we go through these rapid mood identification tips.

Subjunctive. The main sign of the subjunctive is the lengthened connecting vowel (the vowel that comes just before the personal ending in the -ω conjugation). For example, the second person plural present active *indicative* of λύω is λύετε, while the *subjunctive* of the same is λύητε. Notice that the first epsilon became an eta. This lengthening of the connecting vowel is a highly reliable rule for identifying the subjunctive, though it does produce some ambiguous forms.

DAY 19: RAPID MOOD IDENTIFICATION

An easier tip is to look for the words ἵνα, ἀν, and ἐαν. These words are almost always followed by a subjunctive verb. In fact, I like to think of these words as the subjunctive heralds, trumpeting their entrance. It's as if they shout out: Attention! A subjunctive will follow shortly!

One of the very common subjunctive forms is the first person plural subjunctive (the so-called hortatory subjunctive, translated *Let us* . . .). We'll look more closely at these on day 22. For now, we're simply focusing on how to identify the subjunctive. Recall that the ending for first person plural is -μεν. With the lengthened connecting vowel, the ending becomes -ωμεν. Thus, whenever you see a word ending in -ωμεν, you should suspect a hortatory subjunctive. The other possibility, though, is a first person plural indicative from an alpha contract verb, such as ἀγαπάω.

Optative. The optative, as mentioned in an earlier lesson, is quite rare in the New Testament. It is often quite clear from the context that you are looking at an optative. One tip for identifying the optative is that there is usually an unexpected iota or omicron-iota in the place where you would expect the connecting vowel (i.e., just before the personal ending). So, the first person singular present active optative is ἔχοιεν as compared to the indicative of the same, ἔχει.

Imperative and infinitive. These forms have unique endings, so they can be identified directly from the endings. The exception is the second person plural forms of the imperative, which usually look just like the indicative forms of the same Greek word. In this case, the context alone will help you determine whether to understand an indicative or an imperative.

Participle. The two main signs to look for in a participle are a ντ or a μεν just before what otherwise would appear to be a noun or adjective ending. There are a few other participle morphemes, but ντ and μεν are the most common ones. By the way, recall that μεν is also the morpheme for the first person plural personal ending. For the personal ending, of course, it comes at the very end of the word. The participle morpheme μεν always occurs between the verb stem and the ending. You can remember it by saying μεν in the *middle* is a *middle*/passive participle.

Exercise 19

1. Read John 15:10–17. See if you can spot at least twelve subjunctive verb forms.
2. Identify the optative verb form that occurs twice in Rom 3:4–6. Read these verses.
3. Read 1 Cor 14:26–30. Pay special attention to third person imperative forms (third person imperative endings seen in these verses: -σθω, -τω, and -τωσαν).
4. Read Mark 3:23–26. Notice the use of infinitives (infinitive endings seen in these verses: -ειν and -ναι).

Day 20: Finer Points of Tense

The basic idea of each tense was covered in an earlier lesson. Recall these ideas:

Tense	Basic significance
Present	"now" time, ongoing aspect
Imperfect	past time, ongoing aspect
Future	time to come
Aorist	simple past time
Perfect	past action with present consequence
Pluperfect	past action with consequence after the action but ending before the present

In addition to these basic meanings of the tense, there are many other nuances to be learned. However, we will not delve into these advanced topics here. In cases where you need extra input on the tenses, I invite you to consult an intermediate grammar (such as Daniel B. Wallace's *Greek Grammar Beyond the Basics*) or an advanced grammar (such as A. T. Robertson's *A Grammar of the Greek New Testament in Light of Historical Research*). For this lesson, we will look at a few of the most important concepts related to tense.

Present tense. Although all of the tenses can be more complex than the basic ideas suggested above, the present and aorist tenses are the most important ones to consider. For the present tense, the first thing to recognize is that it can also carry the simple (i.e., not ongoing) aspect. For example, consider the English sentence, I eat lunch in the dining hall every day. In a certain sense, this is an ongoing aspect, since the activity began before and continues after the "now" time. But it is probably more accurate to describe this aspect as habitual rather than ongoing. We normally capture ongoing aspect using the -ing ending.

Consider this sentence: I am eating lunch in the dining hall every day. Actually, we would probably consider that sentence to be bad English. It would be ok if we left off the "every day." That is because the -ing construction pictures the event described as happening at the moment of speaking. In a certain sense, the problem is with English. More exactly, English has two different verb forms to capture now-time situations, simple present and present progressive; whereas Greek has only one. Therefore, the one Greek tense is used to capture both ongoing aspect and habitual aspect in the "now" time.

But the Greek present tense can also be used to describe events in times other than the "now." The most important of these is what we call the historical present. This is used, for example, when the narrator wants to draw the readers into the action. In fact, we even use the simple present this way in informal English. For example, you might say: Yesterday we went to the park, and I *see* an old friend and I *say* to him. . . . The historical present (in both Greek and English) tends to make the story seem more immediate and lively.

Aorist tense. Of all the Greek tenses, perhaps aorist is the most discussed in the intermediate and advanced grammars. The probable reason is that we don't have a tense in English that corresponds exactly to the Greek aorist, leaving us to wrestle with the best way to capture the idea of the aorist in the target language. You will see such terms as ingressive aorist or punctiliar aorist. These terms need not detain us here (though they can be helpful for you down the road as you advance in your facility with Greek).

For now, focus in on the basic idea of the aorist: simple or undefined aspect. When we say undefined, that does not mean that the aspect of the aorist is undefined, but that the aspect of a particular verb is not being defined by the author's use of the aorist—aspect is simply not the idea that the author is emphasizing. Here, again, you can try different ways of translating the verb, and select the English form that best captures the simple or undefined aspect.

Tense in non-indicative moods. Another thing to remember about tense—especially present and aorist—is that the time element is mostly gone in the non-indicative moods. In other words, when you encounter a present tense in the subjunctive, optative, imperative, infinitive, or participle moods, that tense does not in itself indicate that the verb describes an event occurring in the "now" time. In the same way, the aorist tense in non-indicative moods does not in itself indicate that a verb describes an event that occurred in the past time. What is most important is the aspect (ongoing for present tense; simple or undefined for the aorist). Of secondary importance is the relative time element. For example, an aorist participle often indicates that the event described by the participle occurred *before* the action of the main verb; while a present participle indicates *simultaneous* action.

Exercise 20

Read John 1:1–13.

1. What are the verb tenses in vv. 1–4?

2. What verb tenses do you find in v. 5? How do you understand the way these verb tenses function? What impact does this have on your understanding of the meaning of the Johannine prologue?

3. Note the tenses in the remainder of this passage. What strikes you here as particularly important?

Day 21: Review—Halfway Home!

Congratulations! You've made it halfway through your forty-day journey to reboot your Greek! I hope you've enjoyed the trip. You started with a fuzzy memory of things studied and forgotten, but you soon re-familiarized yourself with Greek letters and words. You progressed through an overview of the whole noun system. And this week you refreshed your memory of the most important verb forms, i.e., indicative verbs, including all the Greek tenses.

Verb Overview. Starting on day 15, we shifted gears, so to speak. We had been dealing with the noun system, but then we began to look at the mighty Greek verb. The focus on day 15 was not to master the Greek verb system, but to get an overview of the system as a whole. Similarly, on day 16 we focused on an overview of the indicative verb system. These overviews have been and will continue to be especially useful to you as we look at the many verb details. Keeping sight of the "big picture" will help you make sense of the details. Take time now to look back at the diagrams and tables from days 15 and 16.

Tense. Two days this week dealt with verb tenses. Day 17 highlighted the most common signs of each of the Greek tenses. These signs may have been something you missed your first time through studying Greek because (a) they might have gotten lost in all the relentless details and apparent exceptions you had to learn and (b) they take a lot of practice to fully master. Look back at day 17 frequently until you feel like you can handle most verb tenses fairly confidently. Day 20 also looked at tenses, but this time drilling down on some of the syntactical and morphological complexities.

DAY 21: REVIEW—HALFWAY HOME!

Day 18 provided some tips for handling verbs that don't immediately seem to follow expectations ("tricky" verbs). These verbs take even longer than average to master. For now, it is enough to review the tips from this day—while remembering to come back to them from time to time when you feel as if verbs are starting to get the best of you.

Day 19 was important for helping you distinguish between indicative verbs and other verb moods (subjunctive, optative, imperative, infinitive, and participle). Now's a good time to review the tips offered there.

Exercise 21

Reread the passages from the last few exercises. Try to recapture your understanding of those passages that you achieved on the first reading, plus try to stretch your understanding a little bit more. Also try going back to the exercises from day 1. See how far you've come!

Day 22: Finer Points of Mood

Like tense, mood also has a lot of complexities worth delving into. These intricacies can be accessed and studied through the intermediate and advanced grammars, as mentioned on day 20 with respect to tense issues. We won't get bogged down in all the minutiae here, but I do want to mention a few of the more important details that will be especially helpful for reading.

The indicative mood doesn't need our attention here, because it is the most straightforward of the moods. Nor will we talk about infinitive and participle—but for the opposite reason, namely, that they are the most complex of the moods. In fact, we'll look at these two moods in later lessons. The optative mood, because it is rare in the New Testament, need not detain us here either. So, for today, I simply want to mention a few things about the subjunctive and imperative moods.

Subjunctive. We've already noted that the subjunctive mood is the mood of probability or possibility. In other words, it relates to the way that things could be, should be, might be, etc. These are situations that are contingent, which means that for them to come into existence, another circumstance must occur. Consider this sentence: We might go to the beach when the sun comes out. Notice the use of *might go*, which in Greek would correspond to a verb in the subjunctive mood. But in this sentence, going to the beach won't take place unless a condition is met, namely, the sun coming out. Because of the contingency of subjunctive verbs, they are very often preceded by ἵνα or ἄν, words that specifically indicate contingency. Moreover, subjunctives in Greek are usually found in dependent clauses (unlike the example English sentence above, where *might go* is the main verb of the sentence).

DAY 22: FINER POINTS OF MOOD

There is one very common usage of the subjunctive, called the hortatory subjunctive, in which the subjunctive is not a dependent verb. We looked at these briefly on day 19. In the hortatory subjunctive, the speaker (or author) urges the hearers (or readers) to join him or her in a communal or group action. In English, we usually use the *Let us* idiom for this: Let us work very hard so that our goal will be met. In Greek, a single verb in the first person plural subjunctive is used. Consider this example: λέγει τοῖς μαθηταῖς· ἄγωμεν εἰς τὴν Ἰουδαίαν πάλιν (John 11:7b). ἄγωμεν is the first person plural subjunctive of ἄγω, and it is being used as a hortatory subjunctive. We may translate this sentence as *He says to the disciples, "Let us go into Judea again."*

Imperative. The Greek imperative mood is in most respects just like the English imperative—the mood of command. Two things warrant mention here, though. First—and this has nothing to do with Greek or grammar—some people are very uncomfortable with the idea of using the mood of command when addressing God. Their logic is that we cannot command God to do anything, and of course that is true.

But the grammatical mood of command (the imperative) refers to the structure of the sentence (and in the case of Greek, the structure of the word), not to the speaker's heart attitude. The imperative mood is used also for requests, not just commands. So when we address God using the imperative mood, we can either be demanding/commanding or humbly requesting. It's the heart that matters, but the same grammatical form is used for both.

Second, Greek has a third person imperative, which we don't have in English. Often, this form is used when someone (second person) is being asked by the speaker (first person) to make something happen to an inanimate object (third person). For example, in the Lord's prayer ἐλθέτω ἡ βασιλεία σου· γενηθήτω τὸ θέλημά σου can be translated *Cause your kingdom to come; cause your will to be done* (Matt 6:10).

But the third person imperative can also be used of people, as well. This can be for rhetorical effect (Acts 2:36b ἀσφαλῶς οὖν γινωσκέτω πᾶς οἶκος Ἰσραὴλ ὅτι καὶ κύριον αὐτὸν καὶ χριστὸν ἐποίησεν ὁ θεός; *therefore let the whole house of Israel certainly know that God made him both Lord and Christ*), where the speaker does not want to command someone to do something directly.

The third person imperative is also commonly used when the speaker wishes to insist that something happen to an indefinite group or unspecified person (Matt 16:24b εἴ τις θέλει ὀπίσω μου ἐλθεῖν, ἀπαρνησάσθω ἑαυτὸν καὶ ἀράτω τὸν σταυρὸν αὐτοῦ καὶ ἀκολουθείτω μοι; *If people wish to come after me, let them deny themselves and take up their cross and follow me*).[1] In a related use, the speaker may wish to encourage the hearers to resist being forced to do something by a third party (Col 2:16a Μὴ οὖν τις ὑμᾶς κρινέτω; *Do not let anyone judge you*).

Exercise 22

Read the following verses, paying special attention to the use of subjunctives and imperatives.

1. Matt 21:38
2. Mark 9:5
3. Mark 12:14[2]
4. Mark 4:23
5. Mark 15:32
6. 1 Cor 3:18

---

1. I have translated the Greek third person singular verbs and pronouns with the English third person plural to capture accurately the gender-inclusive sense of the original. Note that τις can be either masculine or feminine.

2. You will see the deliberative subjunctive in this verse. The deliberative subjunctive is similar to the hortatory subjunctive, but rather than urging a particular action, it is used to ask the hearers to choose between options.

Day 23: Help with Verb Identification

When I was first starting to read Greek—I remember it clearly to this day—I had difficulty distinguishing between verbs and other parts of speech. When I would encounter unknown words, I would struggle to parse them because I didn't know how to find the word in the lexicon. And I didn't know whether to look for the form on the verb paradigm charts or the noun charts. I remember saying (maybe even out loud), "I wish someone would just tell me whether this is a verb or a noun!"

The first good news for you is that many of the helps available today do exactly that. They tell you what kind of word you are looking at. This greatly simplifies the translation process and makes reading Greek a faster, more enjoyable process. I highly recommend it. There is, however, a little bit of a downside, in that these tools can create an unhealthy dependence. Instead of progressing naturally in your facility with Greek, you can end up stuck at a certain level. You might find that you can't read Greek without looking at your favorite tool for every other word.

But assuming that you do make consistent progress in your ability to read Greek, I can tell you some good news: The difficulty I mentioned above with respect to verb identification really does get easier over time. It gets easier, first, because you become more familiar with a wider vocabulary. So, for instance, you can readily recognize that ἐπῆλθαν is a compound word from ἐπί and ἦλθαν (the third person plural aorist of ἔρχομαι), not an augmented form of an unknown verb πλήθω.

It also becomes easier because you are more familiar with the general sentence structures of Greek and therefore know to expect verbs in certain places. Consider, for example, Acts 14:19 Ἐπῆλθαν δὲ ἀπὸ Ἀντιοχείας καὶ Ἰκονίου Ἰουδαῖοι καὶ πείσαντες τοὺς ὄχλους καὶ λιθάσαντες τὸν Παῦλον ἔσυρον ἔξω τῆς πόλεως νομίζοντες αὐτὸν τεθνηκέναι. Without even knowing the meaning of all the words, an experienced reader expects Ἐπῆλθαν to be an indicative verb because the second καί starts a new clause and there is no other word in the first clause that could be a verb. Similarly, the word ἔσυρον is expected to be a verb because a verb is needed after the dependent participial phrases πείσαντες τοὺς ὄχλους καὶ λιθάσαντες τὸν Παῦλον. But recognizing these things comes with lots and lots of practice. It may seem really difficult right now, but don't be discouraged! If you keep reading, you'll get to the place where these things become almost second nature.

Here are a few observations to help you out in the meantime, as you are working toward building the kind of familiarity mentioned above.

First, know your prepositions because they are often used to form compound words with verbs. Augments (for aorist, imperfect, and sometimes pluperfect) and reduplication (for perfect and pluperfect) come between the preposition and the verb stem. So, if you know your prepositions well, you can quickly see when they're the first part of a word. But don't forget that the prepositions can change their form before a vowel (e.g., δία becomes δι᾽, ἐπί becomes ἐπ᾽, and ἐκ becomes ἐξ). These modified forms often appear in compounded words. Words that begin with ἐπ- are more likely to be a compounded form of ἐπί (673 instances from 104 lexical forms) than an augmented form of a verb that begins with π (471 instances from 53 lexical forms).

Another tricky thing that comes up a lot relates to augments and reduplication. Remember that augments and reduplication can take the form of η instead of the usual ε (for augment) or consonant + ε (for reduplication). This usually happens when the verb begins with an α, ε, or η. For example, the aorist of ἀγαπάω is ἠγάπησα; its perfect is ἠγάπηκα. If you see a word beginning with an η, you should be suspicious that you are looking at an augmented or reduplicated verb.

Also remember that non-indicative forms do not have augments, but perfect-tense verbs do have reduplication. Be aware of

DAY 23: HELP WITH VERB IDENTIFICATION

changes such as ἦλθον (aorist indicative of ἔρχομαι) becoming ἐλθ- in participles and other non-indicative moods.

Finally, remember that the most common verb forms are third person singular (9,427 out of 21,488 total instances exclusive of participles). For comparison, the next most common is third person plural, which has only 3,322 instances. The most common endings for third person singular verbs are these:

1. -εν. This ending occurs 3,618 times as a verb (includes first person plural -μεν). Overall, it occurs 6,985 total times, so more than half the instances are verbs. 2,752 times it is not really an ending at all; it's the whole word, namely, the preposition ἐν. Only 615 times is the ending -εν something else than a verb or the preposition.

2. -ει. The majority of occurrences of this ending are verbs: 1,879 times (usually third person present active indicative, but also including 146 occurrences as second person singular). It also occurs 533 times as a conjunction (usually the particle, εἰ), 328 times as a noun (always a dative singular form), and only 133 times as something else. In total, this ending has 2,873 occurrences.

3. -ται and -νται. 1,547 of the 1,799 total instances are as a verb. Aside from 247 times as a noun, four times as a pronoun, and once as an adjective, the rest are verbs—1,211 times as third person singular, and 336 times as third person plural (in which case it is always -νται).

4. -η. This ending is a little trickier than the other ones on the list because it is more often something other than a verb. It occurs 6,589 times, of which 1,499 are verbs, the majority of which are third person singular (1,322 times). The figures here include the common -θη aorist passive ending.

5. -τιν. At 927 instances, the vast majority of occurrences of this ending in the New Testament are as a third person verb. It occurs as something other than a third person verb just 57 times, in which case it is a noun (accusative singular from a

third declension noun, almost always πίστις). As a third person verb, it is either ἔστιν (from εἰμί, 896 times), ἔξεστιν (28 times), or πάρεστιν (3 times).

6. -το occurs as a verb ending 851 times. 629 of these occurrences are third person singular; the remainder are third plural (always -ντο). However, like the -η ending, -το is more often something other than a verb, occurring 1,694 times as the article τό and 426 times as a pronoun ending.

For those of you with a visual bent, here's a pie chart of these common verb endings:

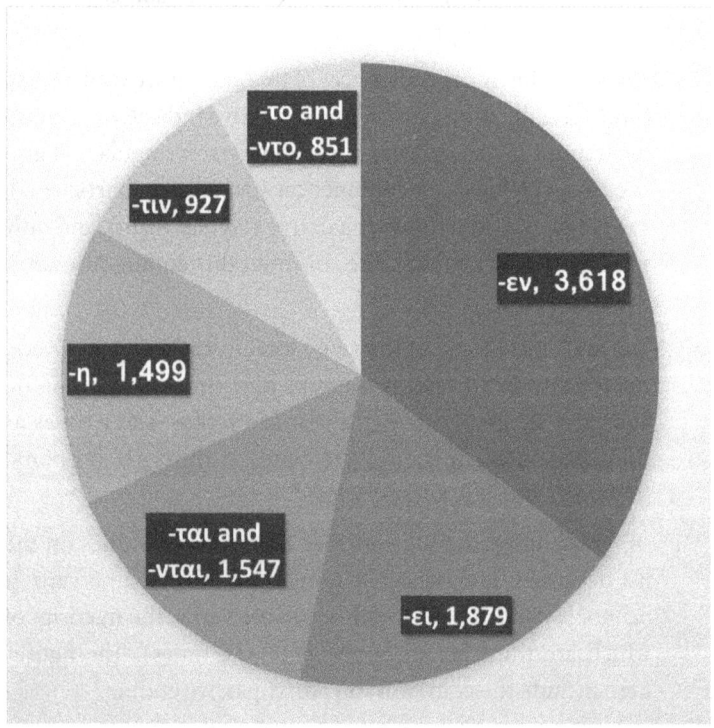

Instances of Common Verb Endings

DAY 23: HELP WITH VERB IDENTIFICATION

Exercise 23

Print out or photocopy the Greek text of John 3. Read through John 3 quickly and mark every word that you think is probably a verb. Now read again more slowly. Are there words that you marked on the first reading that are not verbs? Are there verbs that you missed on the first reading? (Don't worry if you can't get all the way through John 3. As always, just do what time allows.)

1. Are there any patterns that you noticed?
2. What words were hardest to identify? Why?
3. What hints can you lock in your mind to help you with verb identification in the future?

Day 24: Little Words

It's really tempting to ignore the "little words" in Greek. There are a lot of them, and they seem unimportant. But ignoring them is a mistake! Most of the little words are really useful for navigating your way through a sentence. We've already seen how important the article is for helping to identify the function of difficult noun forms in a sentence. For instance, if the word ὁ appears in the sentence, we know that the noun linked to that little word is the subject of the sentence (since ὁ is in the nominative case). As I noted earlier, the article is so important that I highly recommend memorizing all the forms of the article. I don't recommend memorizing all the little words in the same way, but becoming increasingly comfortable with them will make your reading both more rapid and more enjoyable. Little words can often be signposts that help you navigate sentences.

Here are some of the more important "little words."

δέ   This common word is post-positive, meaning it always comes second in the clause. Notice this description (correctly) implies that δέ introduces a new clause. Unlike καί, it is not used to separate phrases or words in a list. Also recall that δέ can mean either *and* or *but*. Although *and* and *but* seem to have opposite meanings in English, in the case of δέ, the same Greek word can carry either idea. It is also possible sometimes to translate δέ with the English word *now*.

ἄν   This little word is often said to be untranslatable. That is more-or-less true, but that doesn't mean the word lacks meaning! As noted on day 19, ἄν is usually used

DAY 24: LITTLE WORDS

to introduce a subjunctive verb. Whenever you see this little word, look for a subjunctive within the next several words of the sentence.

ὅς, ἥ, ὅ   This set of words is easy to confuse with the article. Actually, they are the various nominative singular forms of the relative pronoun (see day 13). The relative pronouns are important for more than just semantics (the meaning of the word). They are also important for indicating the shape of a sentence. A relative pronoun introduces a relative clause. When a relative pronoun appears in a sentence, that sentence is composed (at least) of an *independent* clause with a subject and verb and a *dependent* clause (in this case a relative clause, the one introduced by the relative pronoun). The key to recognizing these words is that they always have a rough breathing mark *and* an accent; they never beginning with a τ. Also notice that the *masculine article* and the *neuter relative pronoun* look very similar. It is easy to mistakenly think that ὁ and ὅ are both nominative masculine singular, but the latter is nominative *neuter* singular.

γάρ   Like δέ, γάρ is post-positive (always coming second in the clause). Meaning *for*, γάρ is used to give the explanation or cause for a preceding statement. For example, John 3:16 begins with the words οὕτως γάρ. In translation, we bring the *For* to the beginning of the sentence. But the word γάρ also invites us to ask how John 3:16 relates to the preceding discussion.

εἰ   This little word is translated *if*. As such, it is used to introduce a conditional statement (e.g., If it rains, the picnic will be canceled). There are some technical details related to different classes of conditional statements, and you should study those whenever the meaning of your passage depends on the specifics of a conditional statement. However, the good news here is that translating the conditionals quite literally into English will usually render their sense quite satisfactorily. So if you are just going for reading and not technical exegesis, you can forego the technicalities.

ἐάν — Like εἰ, this word is translated *if*. It is used for different classes of conditional statements than εἰ (in fact, the use of ἐάν or εἰ is one of the things that identifies the different classes). But, as mentioned above, for reading purposes, you do not need to worry too much about the differences between the classes.

οὖν — Don't mix this word up with the similar-looking preposition σύν. οὖν means *therefore*, and is similar in meaning to γάρ.

καθώς — καθώς is a fairly straightforward "little word." Meaning *just as*, it can be translated quite literally most of the time.

ὥστε — ὥστε indicates result. In other words, it indicates that what is about to follow in the sentence is a result of what was just stated. In John 3:16, we read, *For God so loved the world* ὥστε *he gave*.... God's giving of his son is the result of his loving of the world. There are different ways to capture result in English, so this is a place where you can experiment with different options to see which best captures the statement-result logic.

ἵνα — As indicated in the lesson on the subjunctive (day 19), this word is almost always a sign that a subjunctive is about to come. It is usually translated *in order that*.

DAY 24: LITTLE WORDS

Exercise 24

Read the following verses, paying special attention to how the "little words" shape the structure of the sentences.

1. Matt 18:6–9
2. John 17:12–18
3. 1 Cor 15:11–17
4. Heb 4:5–8

Day 25: Chunking for Success

Perhaps you received the advice early in your first experience with Greek to look first for the subject (nominative case), the verb (indicative mood), and the object (accusative case); then to translate those; and finally to fill out the translation with all the rest of the words in the sentence.

That advice is good, but it only works well for very simple sentences. Most sentences (both in Greek and in English) are complex. In a Greek sentence, there can be many words in the nominative case, in the indicative mood, and the accusative case. And they can come in a wide variety of orders, making translation daunting. I would like to suggest a strategy for dealing with complex sentences, which may be called chunking. This term, chunking, means to break something down into chunks, so that each chunk becomes more manageable.

The basic trick for chunking in this context is to use the little words that we discussed in the last lesson, plus the prepositions. Let's begin with the latter.

Recall that prepositions almost always introduce a prepositional phrase. In Greek, as in English, prepositional phrases consist of a preposition, a very limited number of intervening words, and the object of the preposition. The chunking strategy here is to find all the prepositions in the sentence, together with the objects of those prepositions and the intervening words. Then—in your mind, if not in a physical sense—set that prepositional phrase aside. It becomes a "chunk" in the sentence that you can manipulate as a unit within the translation of the sentence. Notice that—although word order is far less important in Greek than it is in English—prepositional phrases are usually closely bound together as a unit in Greek. That is, the parts of the prepositional

DAY 25: CHUNKING FOR SUCCESS

phrase will generally come very close together in the sentence and other parts of the sentence will not intervene within the phrase except in very limited ways.

Next, use the "little words" to separate the sentence into clauses. As a rule, words can be moved backward or forward within their clause without loss of meaning in Greek; but they cannot be moved into a different clause. Thus, you can chunk whole clauses. Every clause will have a subject (often expressed, but sometimes implicit within the verb) and a verb. Therefore, you can identify the parts of the clause using the aforementioned expedient of identifying subject-verb-(object) within the clause. Then you can move the clauses around in the translated Greek sentence according to the logic of the "little words."

Consider the following examples.

John 6:1

"Unchunked"	Μετὰ ταῦτα ἀπῆλθεν ὁ Ἰησοῦς πέραν τῆς θαλάσσης τῆς Γαλιλαίας τῆς Τιβεριάδος.
"Chunked"	Μετὰ ταῦτα (prepositional phrase: "After these things")
	ἀπῆλθεν ὁ Ἰησοῦς (subject-verb: "Jesus departed")
	πέραν τῆς θαλάσσης (prepositional phrase: "across the sea")
	τῆς Γαλιλαίας τῆς Τιβεριάδος (genitival modifiers: "of Galilee of Tiberias")
Translation	After these things Jesus departed across the sea of Galilee of Tiberias.

John 6:2

"Unchunked"	ἠκολούθει δὲ αὐτῷ ὄχλος πολύς, ὅτι ἐθεώρουν τὰ σημεῖα ἃ ἐποίει ἐπὶ τῶν ἀσθενούντων.
"Chunked"	δὲ (post-positive, moved forward: "And")
	ἠκολούθει αὐτῷ ὄχλος πολύς (subject-verb-object: "large crowd was following him")[1]
	ὅτι ἐθεώρουν τὰ σημεῖα (causal clause: "because they were seeing the signs")
	ἃ ἐποίει (relative clause: "which he was doing")
	ἐπὶ τῶν ἀσθενούντων (prepositional phrase: "upon the ones who were sick")
Translation	And a large crowd was following him because they were seeing the signs which he was doing upon the ones who were sick.

One last piece of advice regarding chunking. You can usually regard an article and the agreeing noun as a chunk. That is to say, usually an article and the agreeing noun will be closely bound together so that the word pair can be chunked in a way comparable to the prepositional phrase mentioned above. There may, however, be intervening words. These intervening words, though, will usually belong to the noun phrase and should be chunked with the article and noun. We discussed this more fully when we talk about "open-faced sandwiches" on day 12.

Exercise 25

The examples in today's lesson were drawn from the beginning of John 6. Continue reading John 6, paying special attention to the structure of each sentence. Use chunking to simplify the sentences into manageable units.

1. Notice the use of the dative αὐτῷ here for the object of the sentence. Some Greek verbs, like ἠκολούθει here, take their objects in the dative case instead of the usual accusative case. No need to memorize which verbs do this, as the context will usually make it clear.

Day 26: To Be (Infinitives)

There are twenty-four forms of every Greek adjective (4 cases times 3 genders times 2 numbers equals 24 forms). Nouns are simpler in a sense because they only come in one gender each. Therefore, there are only eight forms (or sometimes ten) of every noun—ten if you include vocative case.

Infinitives are verbal nouns, and they are simpler than verbal adjectives (i.e., participles—more on them later). In one respect infinitives are even easier than nouns: they aren't inflected for case. So there's only one infinitive form for each tense/voice combination, rather than the expected eight (four cases and two numbers).

In English, the infinitive is formed by using the word *to* plus the simplest form of the verb: *to* eat, *to* talk, *to* play. The passive infinitive adds the word *be* after the *to*, and changes the verb form to past participle (don't ask why!). The passive infinitives of the previous forms would be: to be eaten, to be talked (whatever that might mean), to be played. See the λύω paradigm (appendix B) for the forms of the Greek infinitive. As usual, no need to memorize these forms. Just familiarize yourself with them so that you have a good likelihood of being able to recognize them when you come across them in reading.

Often, the Greek infinitive can be translated using the simple English infinitive. This is true, regardless of the tense of the Greek infinitive, so long as you use the active English infinitive for the Greek active and passive for passive. (For the middle Greek infinitive, use the English active infinitive, perhaps with a few helper words, depending on context.) Here are a few examples.

John 7:1 Καὶ μετὰ ταῦτα περιεπάτει ὁ Ἰησοῦς ἐν τῇ Γαλιλαίᾳ· οὐ γὰρ ἤθελεν ἐν τῇ Ἰουδαίᾳ **περιπατεῖν**, ὅτι ἐζήτουν αὐτὸν οἱ Ἰουδαῖοι **ἀποκτεῖναι**.	And after these things, Jesus was walking in Galilee; for he was not willing **to walk** in Judea, because the Jews were seeking **to kill** him.
John 7:34 ζητήσετέ με καὶ οὐχ εὑρήσετέ [με], καὶ ὅπου εἰμὶ ἐγὼ ὑμεῖς οὐ δύνασθε **ἐλθεῖν**.	You will seek me and you will not find me, and where I am you are not able **to come**.

One of the tricky parts of the Greek infinitive is that it often has the article (e.g., τὸ λαλῆσαι). A word-for-word English translation of this Greek phrase would be, *the to speak*. We would never say, *the to speak*, in English. In fact, we would probably struggle to understand what it actually means. The good news, here, is that you can simply leave the Greek article untranslated without fear of mistranslation. (By the way, some beginners mistake the τό in the above example for the English *to*. They end up translating this phrase correctly, even though they totally miss what is really happening in the Greek.)

You can see an example of the article with the infinitive in Matthew 11:1:

Καὶ ἐγένετο ὅτε ἐτέλεσεν ὁ Ἰησοῦς διατάσσων τοῖς δώδεκα μαθηταῖς αὐτοῦ, μετέβη ἐκεῖθεν **τοῦ διδάσκειν** καὶ **κηρύσσειν** ἐν ταῖς πόλεσιν αὐτῶν.	And it happened when Jesus finished commanding his twelve disciples, he went down from there **to teach** and **to preach** in their cities.

Exercise 26

Some of the examples in today's lesson were drawn from the beginning of John 7. Continue reading John 7, starting in v. 35. Pay special attention to the infinitives in vv. 35–39. As time permits, go back to the beginning of John 7 and read more.

Day 27: To Be Tricky

Yesterday we looked at Greek infinitives. I pointed out that usually you can just translate the Greek infinitive with a simple English infinitive—almost in a one-to-one relationship. Even when the Greek infinitive has an article in front of it, you can still translate with the simple English infinitive—just drop the article.

There are, however, a few other uses of the Greek infinitive that cannot be handled so easily. Most of these tricky syntactical constructions involve the use of prepositions with the infinitive. In these cases, you have to switch the Greek infinitive to an English indicative (and sometimes supply an implied subject). In other words, you just change the Greek infinitive into a regular English verb and don't try to be too literal. It takes some getting used to, but once you get the hang of the usual patterns, it starts to get easier.

Here are some of the common pronoun-infinitive constructions. As usual, no need to memorize.

ἐν + inf. = while	Luke 8:42 Ἐν δὲ τῷ ὑπάγειν αὐτὸν οἱ ὄχλοι συνέπνιγον αὐτόν.	And **while he was going**, the crowds were constricting him.
διά + inf. = because of	Luke 11:8 λέγω ὑμῖν, εἰ καὶ οὐ δώσει αὐτῷ ἀναστὰς **διὰ τὸ εἶναι** φίλον αὐτοῦ . . .	I say to you, even if he will not, getting up, give [anything] to him **because he is** his friend . . .
μετά + inf. = after	Mark 14:28 ἀλλὰ **μετὰ τὸ ἐγερθῆναί με** προάξω ὑμᾶς εἰς τὴν Γαλιλαίαν.	But **after I am raised**, I will go ahead of you into Galilee.

εἰς + inf. = purpose or result	Rom 1:20 ... **εἰς τὸ εἶναι αὐτοὺς** ἀναπολογήτους	... **so that they are** without excuse
πρός + inf. = purpose or result	Eph 6:11 ἐνδύσασθε τὴν πανοπλίαν τοῦ θεοῦ **πρὸς τὸ δύνασθαι ὑμᾶς** στῆναι πρὸς τὰς μεθοδείας τοῦ διαβόλου·	Put on the armor of God **so that you are able** to stand against the tactics of the devil.

Another tricky use of Greek infinitives is that they can have a kind of subject. By definition, infinitives do not have subjects. In practice, however, Greek infinitives can have a subject in a specialized sense. When a Greek speaker (or writer) wanted to indicate the "subject" of an infinitive, they would put that "subject" into the accusative case, not the nominative case. This could occasionally result in a double accusative, one accusative for the "subject" and one for the object. After determining from the context which of the two accusatives is the "subject" and which is the object, we can translate by placing the "subject" into an English prepositional phrase using *for*. Sometimes, the construction can be made clearer by switching to an English indicative with a normal subject.

Consider the following examples:

Acts 15:7 ἐξελέξατο ὁ θεὸς διὰ τοῦ στόματός μου **ἀκοῦσαι τὰ ἔθνη τὸν λόγον** τοῦ εὐαγγελίου καὶ πιστεῦσαι.	God chose **for the Gentiles to hear the word** of the gospel through my mouth and to believe.
Acts 18:5 ... ὁ Παῦλος διαμαρτυρόμενος τοῖς Ἰουδαίοις **εἶναι τὸν χριστὸν Ἰησοῦν**.	... Paul, testifying to the Jews **that Jesus is the Christ**.

One last thing that we should talk about before we leave the topic of infinitives is that they can be used for indirect speech. In English I could say, *Ben said, "I am in the office now."* That is direct speech. But I could say much the same thing using indirect speech: *Ben said that he is in the office now.* To indicate indirect speech in English, we use the word *that* (as opposed to direct speech, which uses a comma and quotation marks). We also change the subject

DAY 27: TO BE TRICKY

and verb from first to third person if necessary. But indirect speech in Greek is indicated—believe it or not—by changing the verbs from whatever mood they were to the infinitive mood. New Testament Greek writers changed the subjects, not from first person to third person, but from nominative to accusative case (just like the "subject" of the infinitive mentioned above).

Here's an example:

Matt 16:15 λέγει αὐτοῖς· ὑμεῖς δὲ τίνα **με** λέγετε **εἶναι**;

Literally: He says to them, "But who do you say **me to be**?"

Better English: He says to them, "But who do you say **I am**?"

Exercise 27

Read Matthew 13:1–9 (or as much as you can accomplish in your allotted time). Pay attention to the infinitives, especially the ones in vv. 4–6.

Day 28: Review

Wow! Time for a breather. We've been on a pretty intense climb over the last week. We started out on day 22 by exploring some of the intricacies of the various Greek verb moods (indicative, subjunctive, optative, imperative, infinitive, and participle). We didn't cover all the moods on those days, though—just subjunctive and imperative. With respect to the subjunctive mood, we noted that it communicates contingency.

We also discussed the hortatory subjunctive, a common use of the subjunctive mood wherein the speaker exhorts his or her hearers to undertake a particular activity (the activity of the verb). For the imperative mood, we discussed its similarity to the English imperative, but also highlighted the third person imperative (which doesn't exist in English). Remember that the third person imperative can be translated using the helping word *let*.

On day 23, I offered some (hopefully) helpful advice on recognizing the verbs in a Greek sentence. I also gave you a list of common word endings and information on how those endings are most commonly used. The idea was to give you strategies for increasing your confidence when encountering new verbs in a passage of the New Testament.

Days 24 and 25 both aimed to give you strategies for reading; that is, moving beyond a word by word plodding through a passage to greater understanding of the shape of any given Greek sentence. Day 24 focused on the little words, which are often overlooked but which frequently give shape to a sentence—and even whole paragraphs of thought. Day 25 talked about chunking, i.e., breaking a sentence into units (phrases, clauses, etc.) that can be taken together to reduce the apparent complexity of longer sentences. Of course, the two strategies of chunking and paying attention to the little words can be used in tandem to increase understanding.

The last two days of the week were devoted to infinitives. On day 26, we noted that most of the time Greek infinitives can be translated with the simple English infinitive. The only tricky thing there was that sometimes the Greek infinitive, because it is by definition a verbal noun, can take an article—something we never do in English. The good news was that we can just leave the Greek article untranslated and use the English infinitive without loss of meaning.

Yesterday we looked deeper at the Greek infinitive. In particular, we discussed the use of infinitives with prepositions, the way to express the "subject" of an infinitive, and the use of infinitives in indirect speech.

Exercise 28

Reread the passages from the last few exercises. Try to recapture your understanding of those passages you achieved on the first reading, plus try to stretch your understanding a little bit more.

Day 29: Power! (Intro to Participles)

Just before yesterday's review, we took two days to look at infinitives, one of the more complex parts of the Greek language. Now we move on to participles, which are probably the most powerful part of the Greek language. So much information is packed into each participle! It is really quite impossible to capture all the information carried by a single Greek participle into a smooth English translation. It usually takes many English words to make a reasonable translation of the Greek, and several more sentences to explain all the stuff that was left out of the translation.

Participles are verbal adjectives. They are part verb and part adjective. As verbs, they can do most everything that verbs can do. They can have tense (present, aorist, perfect, and, rarely, future) and voice (active, middle, and passive). They can have subjects (in a specialized sense) and objects.

But Greek participles can also do what adjectives do, acting attributively or predicatively. They can even act substantively (like a noun). As substantives, they can be the subject or object of clauses and do other nounlike things. And we're not done yet. They can also act adverbially. Yes, participles can "do it all"!

This power comes at a price, though—the price of complexity. Every verb has at least 168 different participle forms! 2 numbers x 3 genders x 4 cases x 7 tense/voice combinations (present active + present middle/passive + aorist active + aorist middle + aorist passive + perfect active + perfect middle/passive). Some verbs also have future participles, making even more forms.

But don't let this complexity scare you! These participle forms are extremely regular, and you already know all the parts that are brought together to form the participles. The active participle morpheme is -ντ-, -υσα-, -κοτ-, or -κυια-, depending on the tense and

DAY 29: POWER! (INTRO TO PARTICIPLES)

gender. The middle/passive morpheme is -μεν- or -θε- (aorist passive only). You might find it helpful to use a mnemonic I picked up from another Greek teacher to help you remember the difference between the -μεν- participle morpheme and the -μεν first person personal ending: *μεν* in the *middle* is the *middle*/passive participle. Consider these two forms: λυόμενος and λύομεν. The former is the middle/passive participle (see the μεν in the middle?) whereas the latter means *we are loosing*.

The participle endings (the number/gender/case indicators) come after the participle morpheme, and they are the endings you already know for the adjectives. They come in two types, one for the active and one for the middle/passive participles. The active participles follow a 3-1-3 pattern, meaning that they follow the third declension for the masculine and neuter forms and the first declension for the feminine forms. The middle/passive participles follow a 2-1-2 pattern. This is the same pattern as the article, so it will be very familiar to you already. (The aorist passive, though, follows a 3-1-3 pattern.)

Study the participle charts in appendix C. As always, look for patterns and repetitions, aiming for familiarity not memorization.

In the next four lessons, we'll look at ways to translate participles. We'll look at what I call the four levels of participle translation. Level 1 is very easy; level 2 is quite easy. Level 3 is where things get a bit tricky. Level 4 is just plain fun after the hard work of level 3 is accomplished.

By the way, it's worth noting here that a level 2 translation is not necessarily better than a level 1 translation. Nor is a level 3 necessarily better than a level 2, and so forth. But you can't know which one is best until you try them all. After going through the process of determining four levels of translation, you may decide that level 1 was the best. But it's the process that makes the choices clear. You're not limited to picking a translation that "just feels right" or that sounds best in English; you can pick the one that best captures the meaning of the Greek.

Exercise 29

Spot the participle(s) in as many of the following verses as time allows. Identify the lexical form of each one.

1. Matt 3:17
2. Matt 4:23
3. Mark 12:42
4. Mark 14:39–40
5. Rom 5:8
6. 1 Cor 2:1
7. 1 Cor 11:25
8. Gal 6:9
9. Eph 2:4
10. Phil 1:27

Day 30: Level 1 Translation

Yesterday we looked at participles. I made the point that there are at least 168 different participle forms for every verb (though not all 168 forms occur in the NT, of course).

That's the bad news. The good news is level 1 participle translation. At level 1, no attempt is made to capture all the complexity of the Greek participle into English. Much of the richness and nuance of meaning is simply smoothed over in favor of making a reasonably accurate translation with relative ease. So the trade-off is power for ease. And level 1 translations are really, really easy. Two-thirds of those 168 forms are translated with a single word, and the remaining one-third are translated with a two-word phrase. To be more specific, the 112 forms of the active and middle participles are all translated with the bare active English participle (____-ing), and the 56 forms of the passive participle are all translated with the English passive participle (being ____-ed).

Consider the following English sentences:

Sleeping, the giant missed his dinner.

The sleeping giant missed his dinner.

In these sentences, the word sleeping is an active participle. In the first sentence, it is acting as an adverbial participle (modifying the verb *missed*), and in the second it is acting as an adjectival participle. But in both cases, the participle is easy to understand and consists of a single word. The passive participle is similar: Being loved, the giant distributed his surplus food to all his neighbors. *Being loved*, of course, is the passive participle.

Now consider these Greek sentences.

- John 18:10 Σίμων οὖν Πέτρος **ἔχων** μάχαιραν εἵλκυσεν αὐτὴν καὶ ἔπαισεν τὸν τοῦ ἀρχιερέως δοῦλον. The word in bold is a present active nominative masculine singular participle. For level 1 participle translations, the only thing we need to know from this parsing is that it is an active participle. As an active participle, we translate with an English active participle. The sentence becomes, *Therefore, Simon Peter,* **having** *a sword, drew it and struck the of-the-high-priest slave* (= . . . *the high priest's slave*).

- John 4:47 οὗτος **ἀκούσας** ὅτι Ἰησοῦς ἥκει ἐκ τῆς Ἰουδαίας εἰς τὴν Γαλιλαίαν ἀπῆλθεν πρὸς αὐτόν. Here the participle is aorist nominative masculine singular. But, again, none of that parsing matters for level 1 translations. We just translate it with a simple active participle: *This one,* **hearing** *that Jesus had come from Judea into Galilee, went to him.*

Tomorrow we'll move up to level 2, where we begin to take account of a little more of the Greek participle power.

Exercise 30

1. Read Luke 19:2–7. Focus on translating the participles using level 1 translations.

2. As time permits, read Matt 26:6–13. Again, use level 1 translations for the participles.

Challenge Bonus: Read 2 Cor 6:3–10, focusing especially on the participles in vv. 9–10.

Day 31: Level 2 Translation

Remember the example that we looked at yesterday:

Sleeping, the giant missed his dinner.

The sleeping giant missed his dinner.

The former sentence can be regarded as an adverbial use of the participle, and the latter as an adjectival use. The distinction is not at all important for the level 1 translations; but it becomes quite important at level 2 and beyond. In Greek, like English, participles can be used either adverbially or adjectivally. A general rule of thumb is that the article is used with adjectival participles and not used with adverbial participles. That's a good place to begin, though you have to keep the possibility in mind that an anarthrous (without article) participle may be adjectival. Practice will really help here.

But let's focus first on the level 2 translations for adverbial participles. At this level, we attempt to capture a little bit more of the richness of the Greek participle, namely, the tense. Recall that there are three primary tenses used with Greek participles: present, aorist, and perfect (future does occur, but rarely). Also remember that the Greek tenses primarily carry aspect and relative time (except in the indicative mood, where past, present, or future time may also be in view).

All that is to say that the tense of Greek participles tells us when the action of the participle took place relative to the action of the main verb (before the main verb for aorist and perfect; at the same time as the main verb for the present). We can capture this relative time element in English translations of adverbial participles by adding a key word to the level 1 translation. Consider these examples (which you'll recognize from yesterday's lesson):

Greek Sentence	Level 1 Translation	Level 2 Translation
John 18:10 Σίμων οὖν Πέτρος **ἔχων** μάχαιραν εἵλκυσεν αὐτὴν καὶ ἔπαισεν τὸν τοῦ ἀρχιερέως δοῦλον.	Therefore, Simon Peter, **having** a sword, drew it and struck the of-the-high-priest slave.	Therefore, Simon Peter, **while having** a sword, drew it and struck the of-the-high-priest slave
John 4:47 οὗτος **ἀκούσας** ὅτι Ἰησοῦς ἥκει ἐκ τῆς Ἰουδαίας εἰς τὴν Γαλιλαίαν ἀπῆλθεν πρὸς αὐτόν.	This one, **hearing** that Jesus had come from Judea into Galilee, went to him.	This one, **after hearing** that Jesus had come from Judea into Galilee, went to him.

As you can see, level 2 translations are also quite easy, but not quite as easy as level 1. With level 1 translations, you only have to recognize that a word is a participle and translate the word using the -ing form (for active; -ed for passive). At level 2, you have to recognize two additional pieces of information: (1) adverbial v. adjectival and (2) tense. Once those two pieces are discerned, level 2 is simple for adverbial. We'll hold off on level 2 adjectival until day 34.

But back to level 2 translations for adverbial participles. Once you've identified that the participle you are working on is being used adverbially (usually one that does not have an article), make note of the tense. If it is an aorist or perfect participle, simply add *after* to the level 1 translation. If the participle is present, add *while* to the level 1 translation.

Exercise 31

Look back at the verses you read yesterday and the day before (days 29 and 30). Identify the participles, and this time translate them using level 2 translations.

Day 32: Level 3 Translation

When people cringe at the thought of translating Greek participles, it may be because they try to handle all the complexity in one single step. It's a bit like trying to eat a whole apple with a single bite—it's just too much to handle that way. That's why I've tried to simplify the process by breaking it down into "bite-sized" chunks. We began with what I call level 1 translation, which really only requires you to recognize that the word you are trying to translate is a participle. Level 2 translations require you to recognize the participle, and also to account for the tense of that participle. So you've got two bites, each with a single bit of information to handle.

Level 3 translations are significantly harder to manage. Unfortunately, there's no way to further break down this translation level and still end up with a workable translation at the end. Nevertheless, level 3 translations still only process two additional pieces of information, namely, the "subject" of the participle and the time relationship between the participle and the main verb. The good news, though, is that once you have handled this "biggest bite," you've accomplished the hardest part of participle translation.

Level 4 translations are a lot easier than level 3—but you can't do them without first having done level 3 translations. With that in mind, let's dig in to level 3! As you go through the remainder of today's lesson, you may find it helpful to follow the participle flowchart in appendix D, which traces all the translation steps visually.

Grammarians will likely cringe when I talk about the "subject" of a participle. That's why I usually put the word *subject* in quotes in the phrase, "subject" of a participle. This indicates that we're just calling it a subject, when technically it's something else. But here in level 3 we're basically transforming what in Greek is a verbal phrase into a dependent clause in English. And when we're dealing with clauses, it really is appropriate—even necessary—to talk about subjects. All that is to say, we've got to find the referent of the participle in Greek and add a pronoun in English to supply the function of subject in our new English clause.

This task is usually simpler than the preceding paragraph made it sound! The "subject" of the participle is the noun or pronoun with which the participle agrees in gender, number, and case. So for example, in the Greek sentence Σίμων οὖν Πέτρος ἔχων μάχαιραν εἵλκυσεν αὐτὴν καὶ ἔπαισεν τὸν τοῦ ἀρχιερέως δοῦλον (John 18:10, from yesterday and the day before), the participle ἔχων (having) agrees with the noun Σίμων Πέτρος (Simon Peter), so Σίμων Πέτρος is the "subject" of ἔχων—and also the subject (no scare quotes; it really is the subject this time). Therefore, we add the pronoun *he* (where he refers to Simon Peter) to our participle translation.

Also note that often the "subject" of the participle is the subject of the sentence. In this situation, the participle will be in the nominative case. And it is common that the subject of the sentence is unexpressed, being embedded within the verb. So it is possible for a nominative participle not to have an agreeing noun or pronoun. Here's an example:

Mark 1:39 Καὶ ἦλθεν **κηρύσσων** εἰς τὰς συναγωγὰς αὐτῶν εἰς ὅλην τὴν Γαλιλαίαν καὶ τὰ δαιμόνια **ἐκβάλλων**.

Level 1: And he went **preaching** into their synagogues into the whole Galilee and **casting out** the demons (= And he went into the whole Galilee preaching into their synagogues and casting out demons).

Level 2: And he went **while preaching** . . . and **while casting out** demons.

Level 3: And he went **while he** . . . and **while he** . . .

Adding the pronoun is the first half of the two-part level 3 translation process. It is fairly straightforward, but it doesn't

DAY 32: LEVEL 3 TRANSLATION

finish the job. In the sentence, ἔρχεται οὖν καὶ Σίμων Πέτρος ἀκολουθῶν αὐτῷ (John 20:6), the level 1 translation would be *Therefore, Simon Peter also came following him*. The level 2 translation would be *Therefore, Simon Peter also came while following him*. But level 3 translation cannot be *Therefore, Simon Peter also came while he following him*.

Once we add the pronoun, we also have to change the participle to a regular verb. To do so, first recall that a present participle occurs at the same time as the main verb. So to catch the English tense of the participle-to-verb conversion, you must check the tense of the main verb. If the main verb is present tense, the tense of the participle-to-verb conversion is also present; if the main verb is past, the participle-to-verb conversion is also past; and so forth. In the John 20:6 example above, the correct level 3 translation would be *Therefore, Simon Peter also came to him while he was following him*.

For aorist participles, the action of the participle is prior to the action of the main verb, and you must select the tense of the participle-to-verb conversion accordingly. If the main verb is past, the *aorist* participle-to-verb conversion will be perfect; if the main verb is present, the *aorist* participle-to-verb conversion will be past; and so forth.

Also, the present participle indicates ongoing action, so the aspect in English should normally be progressive. For aorist participles, on the other hand, the aspect is simple or undefined, so the aspect in English should usually be simple.

Study the following examples:

Acts 13:11 καὶ νῦν ἰδοὺ χεὶρ κυρίου ἐπὶ σὲ καὶ ἔσῃ τυφλὸς μὴ βλέπων τὸν ἥλιον ἄχρι καιροῦ.

> L1: And now, behold; the Lord's hand is upon you and you will be blind, not seeing the sun for a time.
>
> L2: . . . while not seeing . . .
>
> L3: . . . while you will not see . . .

Matt. 26:27 καὶ λαβὼν ποτήριον καὶ εὐχαριστήσας ἔδωκεν αὐτοῖς λέγων· πίετε ἐξ αὐτοῦ πάντες,

L1: And taking a cup and giving thanks, he gave [it] to them saying, "All of you drink from it."

L2: And after taking a cup and after giving thanks, he gave [it] to them while saying, "All of you drink from it."

L3: And after he took a cup and gave thanks, he gave [it] to them while he said, "All of you drink from it."

Exercise 32

Look one more time at the translations from days 29 and 30. This time, translate the participles using level 3 translations.

Day 33: Level 4 Translation

Congratulations on making it through the hardest part of participle translation (level 3)! Welcome to the most fun part of participle translation (level 4)! Level 4 builds on level 3, but for the most part, it is just a matter of swapping out one word, namely, the *while* or *after* that begins the level 3 clause.

Level 2 and level 3 operate under the assumption that all participles are temporal in nature, that is, that their primary function is to indicate a time relationship between the action of the participle and the action of the main verb. While many participles—perhaps even most participles—are indeed temporal, that is certainly not the only logic that participles can carry. Participles could be causal, concessive, conditional, and more. Here's a chart complete with a description and example of each option. Pay special attention to the way that level 3 is modified to create each level 4 variant.

Option	Description	Greek Example	Level 3 Translation	Level 4 Translation
Temporal (= level 3)	Same as level 3. Participle tells when an action takes place. Use *while*, *after*, or *when*.	Mark 10:47 And ἀκούσας that it was Jesus the Nazarene, he began to cry out and say, "Jesus, Son of David, have mercy on me."	And *after he heard* that it was Jesus . . .	And *after he heard* that it was Jesus . . . (no change)

Option	Description	Greek Example	Level 3 Translation	Level 4 Translation
Causal	Indicates why an action takes place. Use *because* or *since*.	John 6:15 Therefore, Jesus γνούς that they were about to come and arrest him to make him king, withdrew again to the mountain alone.	Therefore, Jesus, *while he knew* that they were about to...	Therefore, Jesus, *because he knew* that they were about to...
Conditional	Indicates the condition for an action taking place. Use *if*.	Gal 6:9 Let us not become weary in doing good, for at the proper time we will reap a harvest μὴ ἐκλυόμενοι (TNIV)	... we will reap a harvest *while we do* not *give up*.	... we will reap a harvest *if we do* not *give up*.
Concessive	Denotes a sense of concession, i.e., conceding a point but maintaining the truth of a statement nevertheless. Use *though* or *although*.	Gal 4:1 Now I say, as long as the heir is a child, he does not differ at all from a slave κύριος πάντων ὤν (NASB)	... he does not differ at all from a slave *while he is master of all things*.	... he does not differ at all from a slave *although he is master of all things*.

DAY 33: LEVEL 4 TRANSLATION

Option	Description	Greek Example	Level 3 Translation	Level 4 Translation
Instrumental	Indicates the means by which the action of the main verb is accomplished. Use *by means of* or *by*.	Phil 2:8 He humbled himself γενόμενος obedient until death.	He humbled himself *while he became* . . .	He humbled himself *by becoming* . . .
Purpose	Indicates the purpose for an action taking place. English usually captures purpose with an infinitive, so you can switch to infinitive construction here. Use *to* or *in order to* + infinitive.	Matt 1:19 And Joseph her husband, being righteous and not θέλων to disgrace her, planned to divorce her quietly.	. . . being righteous and *while he was* not *wanting* to disgrace her . . .	. . . being righteous and *in order to* not disgrace her . . .
Result	Indicates the result of an action taking place. Use *with the result that*.	Matt 8:27 And the people were amazed λέγοντες, "What sort is this person that even the winds and the sea obey him?"	. . . were amazed *while they were saying* . . .	. . . were amazed *with the result that they were saying* . . .

105

Option	Description	Greek Example	Level 3 Translation	Level 4 Translation
Manner	Indicates the way in which the action of the main verb took place. Use *in the manner of*. Sometimes best left at level 1.	Matt 7:29 For he was teaching them as ἔχων authority and not as their scribes.	For he was teaching them *while he had* authority...	For he was teaching them *in the manner of having* authority...
Attendant Circumstance	Indicates that an action took place along with the main verb action. Use *and*.	Eph 2:17 And ἐλθὼν he preached peace to you who were far and peace to the ones who were near.	And *while he came*, he preached...	And he came and preached...

I said earlier that level 4 is the most fun part of participle translation. The reason is that there is a lot of room for discussion about which of the options best captures the logic of the sentence. So go ahead and *play around* (play = fun!). Try replacing the *while* or *after* from a level 3 translation with each of the level 4 options in turn (turn = play!). The good news here is that the internal sentence logic doesn't change between Greek and English here, so you can do all your playing in English. Enjoy!

Exercise 33

Look for one last time at the translations from days 29 and 30. This time, translate the participles using level 4 translations.

Day 34: Level 2a Translation

For today's lesson, we circle back and pick up a whole different kind of participle. So far, all the participles we have been looking at (other than a brief mention) have been the adverbial type. The other option, the one we zoom in on today, is the adjectival type. There are basically only two ways to translate adjectival participles, level 1 and level 2a. As this nomenclature implies, level 1 is the same for both adverbial and adjectival participles (remember, level 1 translation consists of the bare English participle, nothing more). I call the second adjectival translation level 2a, though, to distinguish it from the regular level 2 translation, which is for adverbial participles only. Also notice that there is no such thing as level 3a or level 4a. Once you've mastered level 2a, you've got it all for adjectival participles.

At this point, it is helpful to recall the rule of thumb mentioned earlier regarding how to distinguish between adverbial and adjectival participles. Adjectival participles usually have an article, while adverbial participles "never" do. I add the scare quotes to the *never* because, with language, it's dangerous to make absolute statements. But this principle is pretty reliable. If you see an article before the participle, you are pretty safe to proceed under the expectation that you are looking at an adjectival participle. On the other hand, if neither the participle nor the agreeing noun has an article, then it is possible that this is still an adjectival participle.

To get us into how level 2a works, I want to point out that participles and relative clauses have a lot of overlap in terms of what they are trying to communicate in a sentence. Consider the following examples.

Participle	Relative Clause
The sleeping giant...	The giant who sleeps...
The written word...	The word that was written...

Both the participial construction and the clausal construction communicate the same (or at least very similar) ideas. The participial construction is used a lot in Greek because the Greek participle is so powerful. But to catch more of that power in English translation, we have to switch over to relative clauses. It is uncommon in English to add anything to the participle construction beyond the participle itself. We rarely add helping verbs, objects, or modifiers to the participle. But we often do that for relative clauses. For example, we could say any of the following:

- The giant who is sleeping...
- The giant who was sleeping... (not: the was-sleeping giant)
- The giant who has been sleeping... (not: the has-been-sleeping giant)
- The giant who slept until dawn... (not: the who-slept-until-dawn giant)
- The giant who ate the super-sized pumpkin pie... (not: the who-ate-the-super-sized-pumpkin-pie giant).

The flexibility that English has with the relative clause is available to Greek using the adjectival participle. If the Greek sentence is quite simple, you can translate the adjectival participle at level 1. But more often, you will need to move up to level 2a, which entails transforming the Greek participial phrase into an English relative clause.

The good news here is that in many respects this transformation follows a similar pattern to what we have already talked about for level 3: (1) add a pronoun that agrees with the "subject" of the participle and (2) transform the participle into a regular verb. Step 1 is actually slightly easier for adjectival participles than for adverbial participles: simply choose "who" or "whom" if the

DAY 34: LEVEL 2A TRANSLATION

participle refers to a person or "which" if the participle refers to a thing. Step 2 for adjectival participles is identical to adverbial participles. For present participles: if the main verb is present, choose present progressive for the transformation; if the main verb is aorist, choose past progressive; and so forth. For aorist participles: if the main verb is present, choose simple past for the transformation; if the main verb is aorist, choose perfect; and so forth. Again, see appendix D for a flowchart that captures all this complexity in a simple visual format.

One more thing before I let you go for today. As I said before, Greek participles are very powerful. They're verbs, so they can do everything that a verb can do. They can function adverbial, so they can do what adverbs do. And they are adjectives, so they can do everything that adjectives can do—including acting like nouns! Adjectives can function substantively, taking the place of a noun. For example, in the sentence, "The hungry will be satisfied," hungry is an adjective acting as the subject of the sentence. If we want to spell it out, we could say, "The hungry people will be satisfied."

It gets complicated, though, when we switch to a participle. For example, "The running will be stopped" and "The running people will be stopped" do not mean exactly the same thing. In Greek, substantive participles work in the latter way, not the former. For example, in the clause, ὁ ζητῶν εὑρίσκει (Matt 7:8), a level 1 translation would be, the seeking finds. But really, we need to add the word *person:* the seeking person finds. Or better yet, switch to a relative clause: the person who seeks finds.

Exercise 34

As time allows, translate as many of the following verses as possible, first using a level 1 translation, then moving to a level 2a translation.

1. Matt 6:4
2. Luke 11:10
3. John 3:16
4. John 5:37
5. John 6:57
6. Rom 8:11
7. Rom 10:5

Day 35: Review

This week has been all about participles. If you were like most beginning Greek students, you struggled mightily with participles the first time through. That was probably due to two factors: morphology and syntax. Beginning students tend to make the morphology of participles harder than it needs to be. Remember that participles have the marks of tenses (lexical form for present, σα for aorist—but no augment, which is only used in the indicative mood—and, usually, reduplication for perfect). Then participles have a participle morpheme, followed by adjective endings. Once you master this participle formula, the morphology is pretty straightforward—especially as you become more and more comfortable with third declension endings, which are used for active participles.

The syntax of participles is more difficult to handle. This difficulty arises out of the sheer power of the Greek participle. Handling Greek participles is a little bit like using a fire hydrant hose when you've been accustomed to watering plants with a garden hose—you'll get wet if you're not careful!

Days 30–34 were devoted to helping you relearn how to handle all this participial power, one step at a time. We started with level 1 translations, which exchange power for simplicity. Level 1 translations work pretty well most of the time, but they fail to capture much of the richness that Greek participles convey. Level 2 translations add a little bit more of the power but still leave a lot of the meaning unexpressed. Basically, this level adds awareness of the participle tense but not much else. Level 3 translations are where the hardest translation work takes place. At this level, you have to deal with, not just the participle itself, but also with the grammatical relationship between the participle and the rest of the sentence (this happens also to some extent at level 2a, which we looked at yesterday).

Though level 3 translations are difficult at first, they are really satisfying because you are able to account for most of the multifaceted information embedded in the participle form. They also prepare you for level 4 translations. At level 4, you retain most of the information gathered from level 3, but you go beyond that to consider, not just grammatical relationships, but also the semantic relationship between the participle and the main verb. Level 4 translations begin to move from translation to interpretation.

As you master the levels of participle translation, your participle muscles will become strong enough to handle all their power. Don't be discouraged if you get confused from time to time. It takes lots of practice to build up your muscles. But the rewards are great if you keep at it.

Oh, and by the way, we're not yet done with all the participial possibilities! That's what day 36 and day 37 are for!

Exercise 35

Reread the passages from the last few exercises. Try to recapture your understanding of those passages that you achieved on the first reading, plus stretch your understanding a little bit more.

Day 36: Genitive Absolute

Genitive absolute ... the very words strike fear into the heart of many a Greek student! For starters, the component terms seem mystifying: you've just begun to get a handle on the genitive, and now words in the genitive case are doing something new and different! And what's this about absolute—what kind of grammatical term is that? Sounds absolutely mysterious. Today we'll focus on demystifying this mystery.

Let's start with the term *absolute*. The basic idea is that you've got two thoughts expressed in a single sentence with no grammatical connection between them. Consider the following two sentences:

After he ate breakfast, the violinist played a symphony.

After the drummer ate breakfast, the violinist played a symphony.

In the first sentence, there is a grammatical link between the two clauses (he = the violinist). But in the second clause, there is no link (the drummer ≠ the violinist). In English, we handle this situation quite seamlessly using adverbial clauses, as in the above examples. But recall that Koine Greek speakers often preferred participial phrases. The first sentence above could easily be handled using an aorist nominative participle (aorist to capture the "after," and nominative to connect the "subject" of the participle to the violinist, i.e., the subject of the main clause).

But in the second sentence, you couldn't use a nominative participle because that would imply that the drummer and the violinist were the same person. Nor could you use an accusative participle, because that would imply that the drummer was a symphony! The Greeks solved this little problem by using a genitive

DAY 36: GENITIVE ABSOLUTE

participle and placing the otherwise unconnected "subject" of the participle also in the genitive.

It all makes sense when you think about it. The "subject" of the genitive participle is the noun or pronoun in the genitive case. The problem comes when Greek students forget about the existence of this little Greek trick. They are reading along in their Greek New Testaments and come to a word in the genitive. Automatically, they translate "of ____." Then they begin looking around for some other noun to which they should connect the "of" phrase. They may or may not find a candidate for that. But when they move on to the participle and try to add "of ___ing" to the sentence, they end up totally confused.

The antidote is simply to remember that when you encounter a genitive participle, it very well might be a genitive absolute construction, in which case the usual "of" is no longer needed because the genitive is being borrowed to do a job outside its normal possessive functions.

Here are some examples.

Luke 7:24a Ἀπελθόντων δὲ τῶν ἀγγέλων Ἰωάννου ἤρξατο λέγειν πρὸς τοὺς ὄχλους περὶ Ἰωάννου· τί ἐξήλθατε εἰς τὴν ἔρημον θεάσασθαι; And *after the messengers* of John *departed*, he began to say to the crowds concerning John, "What did you go out into the desert to see?"

Acts 10:44 Ἔτι λαλοῦντος τοῦ Πέτρου τὰ ῥήματα ταῦτα ἐπέπεσεν τὸ πνεῦμα τὸ ἅγιον ἐπὶ πάντας τοὺς ἀκούοντας τὸν λόγον. While *Peter was still saying* these words, the Holy Spirit fell upon all the ones hearing the word.

Exercise 36

Translate as many of the following verses as time allows.

1. John 6:23
2. Acts 19:6
3. Rom 7:9
4. Gal 3:25
5. Mark 6:22
6. Acts 18:14
7. 1 Thess 3:6

Day 37: So That's Why We Do It! (Periphrastic Construction)

When I was in elementary school, we used to talk about helping verbs. That was a long time ago, and I don't know if they still use that terminology with children these days. But the idea is somewhat useful for understanding today's topic. In English, helping verbs are the "to be" and "have" verbs that are added to the main verb to form a new tense. For example, in the sentence, "I am eating," the *am* is a helping verb. What I was never told in elementary school (so far as I can remember, at least) is that the verb to which the *am* is added is in the form of a participle! Think about it: how do you get an active participle? Add -ing (as in *eating*, in the example sentence). You can also use a passive participle with a helping verb: I was washed. Note that the passive participle with a *to be* helping verb is the standard way that we form the passive voice in English.

But let's focus on the use of the active participle with a "to be" helping verb: I was eating, I have been eating, I am eating, I will be eating. The combination of "to be" with the participle gives a sense of duration to the action, called "imperfective aspect" by grammarians. The tense of the *to be* verb determines the time element of the verb complex: *was* for past time, *have been* for perfect, *am* for present, and *will be* for future.

Turning to Greek, there are non-helping verb ways to formulate these time/aspect combinations. But Greek can also utilize the "to be" verb with participles in much the same way as English. In fact, most of the time you can just translate word-for-word! In Greek, we call this the periphrastic construction. Here are some examples.

DAY 37: SO THAT'S WHY WE DO IT! (PERIPHRASTIC CONSTRUCTION)

Luke 4:31 Καὶ κατῆλθεν εἰς Καφαρναοὺμ πόλιν τῆς Γαλιλαίας. καὶ *ἦν διδάσκων* αὐτοὺς ἐν τοῖς σάββασιν. And he came down into Capernaum, a city of Galilee, and *he was teaching* them on the Sabbath.

Luke 11:14 Καὶ *ἦν ἐκβάλλων* δαιμόνιον [καὶ αὐτὸ ἦν] κωφόν· ἐγένετο δὲ τοῦ δαιμονίου ἐξελθόντος ἐλάλησεν ὁ κωφὸς καὶ ἐθαύμασαν οἱ ὄχλοι. And *he was casting* out a demon and it was mute; and it happened, after the demon came out, the mute person spoke and the crowds were amazed. [Note also the genitive absolute in this sentence.]

Exercise 37

Translate as many of the following verses as time allows.

1. Matt 7:29
2. Matt 19:22
3. Mark 5:5
4. Luke 4:44
5. Luke 15:24
6. Acts 21:33
7. Heb 2:13

Day 38: Tools: Lexica and Parsing Guides

In the introduction to this book, I mentioned that I would give you several tools that would make it easier to read Greek with greater speed, and therefore give you a higher probability of continuing to read on a regular basis. I already introduced you to one of the best tools for this (*GNT Reader's Edition*) back on day 2. Today I want to introduce (or reintroduce, as the case may be) you to a few more tools that can be of great help to you as you continue making progress in NT Greek.

One of the most important tools you will need as you progress in reading and studying Greek is a lexicon (pl: lexica). A lexicon, in simplest terms, is a dictionary that describes the meaning of the words of a given language. A New Testament Greek lexicon, for instance, describes the Greek words that occur in the New Testament. For our purposes, the description is given in English. But, of course, there are also Greek lexica in German, French, and so forth.

There are many lexica to choose from, but all are not of the same quality. For instance, one very easily accessible lexicon is Thayer's Lexicon available online at www.blueletterbible.org (more on Blue Letter Bible later). There is a lot of important information available in this lexicon, but there is one major problem: it's outdated. Created over one hundred years ago, this lexicon was state-of-the-art when it was written. But in the intervening years, our understanding of the Koine Greek language has advanced exponentially. Two key developments led to these advancements: (1) the discovery of the ancient papyri at Oxyrhynchus, Qumran, and elsewhere and (2) progress in the understanding of the nature of words. In the latter case, for example, since Thayer's work was completed there has been a growing understanding of the distinction between a gloss (merely replacing a Greek word with an English one) versus precise definitions.

DAY 38: TOOLS: LEXICA AND PARSING GUIDES

Let's focus on perhaps the two most important lexica available to the serious student today. First up is Bauer, Danker, Arndt, and Gingrich's *Greek-English Lexicon of the New Testament and Other Early Christian Literature* (aka BDAG).[1] Now in its third English edition, BDAG is still considered the gold standard for serious study of the meaning of Greek words. The strength of BDAG is the writers' encyclopedic knowledge of a broad scope of the extant Koine Greek documents. They often cite extrabiblical sources to illuminate the meaning of words. When utilizing BDAG, don't skip over the references to Homer and Plato, or Josephus and Plutarch, as these are invaluable references for understanding the language—even if just to get a sense of the history of the word.

The second lexicon I would mention is *Greek-English Lexicon of the New Testament Based on Semantic Domains*, edited by Johannes P. Louw and Eugene A. Nida, usually referred to simply as Louw and Nida.[2] This work is organized by synonyms (i.e., semantic domains), rather than in alphabetical order as most lexica. Louw and Nida represents two significant advances in lexicography.[3] First, it attempts actual definitions rather than mere glosses. This allows translators to be more accurate in selecting the right words in their target languages to capture the intent of the original writer. Second, by arranging according to synonyms, it becomes much easier to see how a given word is related to similar words, clearly conveying in what ways is it like and how is it distinct from similar words. Again, this feature provides a significant benefit to translators and readers.

One of the challenges of using these two lexica is actually finding the listing for your word. Often, especially for nouns,

---

1. Walter Bauer, Frederick W. Danker, William Arndt, and F. Wilbur Gingrich, *Greek-English Lexicon of the New Testament and Other Early Christian Literature*, 3rd ed. (Chicago: University of Chicago Press, 2000).

2. Johannes P. Louw and Eugene A. Nida, eds., *Greek-English Lexicon of the New Testament Based on Semantic Domains*, 2nd ed. (New York: United Bible Societies, 1989).

3. Constantine R. Campbell, *Advances in the Study of Greek: New Insights for Reading the New Testament* (Grand Rapids: Zondervan, 2015), Kindle edition, 44.

pronouns, and adjectives, the process is straightforward. But because of augments, reduplication, and other prefixes—not to mention the idiosyncrasies of second aorists and "irregular" verbs—it can be a challenge to find the lexical form of verbs.

Three things can help. First, use a process of elimination. If you don't find a word that begins with an epsilon in the epsilon section of the lexicon, assume that that epsilon is an augment—therefore look under the consonant that occurs right after the epsilon. Similarly, if a word begins with an eta but is not in the eta listings, assume that the eta is an augmented (lengthened) vowel. Check under alpha or epsilon.

Second, learn the common prepositions. Remember that the augment and reduplication come between the prepositional prefix and the stem. Once you know the common prepositions, you can more easily recognize when an augment or reduplication is present in what appears to be the middle of a word. Third, if you still can't find your word in the lexicon, use one of the many parsing guides that are available. (More on this in a moment.)

One word of caution before we leave this topic. Preachers are often allured by the prospect of painting word pictures to spice up their sermons and wow their audience with their knowledge of the Greek. Quite aside from the spiritual considerations relative to trying to impress people, the question must be raised as to whether the approach itself is fundamentally flawed. To be more precise, never lose sight of the fact that the immediate context of a word is the most important consideration for determining how that word is being used. Ask: is the information about your word gleaned from the lexicon actually present in this passage? Sometimes, the word picture can be a distraction from the point the Biblical writer was trying to make rather than enhancing our understanding.

I mentioned that there are guides to help you identify the parsing of the words of the New Testament. Some include both nouns and verbs; others include just the verbs. In both cases, these tools can really help out when you get stumped on the meaning and use of a word. These tools can be divided into two kinds: print-based and computer-based.

DAY 38: TOOLS: LEXICA AND PARSING GUIDES

Perhaps the most accessible print-based parsing guide is the resource already mentioned earlier, namely, the *Reader's Edition Greek New Testament*. The great advantage of this volume is that the complete text of the New Testament is the center of attraction, so to speak—no need to carry along a second volume (the text and the guide). Of course, not every word is parsed; in fact, nouns are not parsed at all (though enough of the lexical information is given so that you can easily complete the parsing in most cases). A disadvantage (or advantage, depending on your perspective) is that the common verbs (i.e., verbs occurring more than thirty times in the NT) are not parsed. On the other hand, tricky verb forms (such as second aorists) are parsed even for those that are common.

If you find that the parsing of the *Reader's Edition* is not sufficient for you needs (a circumstance that is likely to become less frequent as you gain familiarity with the Greek through use over time), you might also consult Nathan E. Han's *A Parsing Guide to the Greek New Testament* or Maximilian Zerwick's *A Grammatical Analysis of the Greek New Testament*.[4]

Many people these days will find it more convenient to choose a computer-based parsing guide rather than one of the print-based tools mentioned above. More on this tomorrow.

Exercise 38

1. Look up BDAG, Louw and Nida, Han's *Parsing Guide*, and Zerwick's *Grammatical Analysis* at one of your favorite online book resellers (unless, of course, you already own one or more of them). Get a feel for what each one aims to provide its users. Do a quick cost-benefit analysis on each. Which would you consider buying, if any?

2. Read Ephesians 2:1–11, making note of any words you might wish to look up in a lexicon or parsing guide.

---

4. Nathan E. Han, *A Parsing Guide to the Greek New Testament*, reissue ed. (Harrisonburg, VA: Herald, 1994), and Maximilian Zerwick, *A Grammatical Analysis of the Greek New Testament*, trans. Mary Grosvenor, 5th ed. (Rome: Biblical Institute Press, 1996).

Day 39: Tools: Bible Software

There are many computer-based resources for helping with Greek. I'm not going to attempt a review of all the resources that are available; I just want to mention some of the more important resources and suggest a few tips for how make the most of them for continuing with your Greek long term. For most resources, I will not provide web addresses, which tend to change. Simply do an online search for the item by name (for example, SBLGNT), and you will easily find what you are looking for.

Yesterday I mentioned blueletterbible.org and some of the resources there. This website is great for getting started with word studies, but it is limited beyond that. The key to using Blue Letter Bible for word studies is to make sure to click the checkbox next to "Strong's" on the menu bar. Start by entering the reference of a verse that contains the word you want to study into the search box on the Blue Letter Bible home page. (Be sure to select either KJV or NASB as the version, as only these two allow you to search using Strong's numbers.)

On the resulting search results page, click the Strong's checkbox, and Strong's numbers will appear next to all the words in the text. Now, simply click on the number next to your word, and a new page will appear. Scroll down past Thayer's lexicon entry for your word to the Concordance Results section. Here you can read (in English translation) every instance of your word in the New Testament. Reading these verses allows you to get a good, firsthand feel for the denotations and connotations of your word.

Another great free resource is the Society of Biblical Literature's Greek New Testament (SBLGNT). This text of the NT differs slightly from the more widely accepted text (Nestle-Aland), but is very usable for most purposes. Certainly, you can use it for

DAY 39: TOOLS: BIBLE SOFTWARE

your daily Greek reading. It can also be used for basic text-critical purposes. It includes a text-critical apparatus, but the apparatus refers only to variants within printed texts, not the actual Greek manuscripts. The SBLGNT is available in a variety of file formats. The easiest one to access is the pdf format, while the most versatile one is the Logos format. The Logos format, however, requires the use of the Logos Bible Software program—which brings us to our next topic.

There are three widely used, highly regarded Bible software programs: Logos Bible Software, BibleWorks,[1] and Accordance. Except for BibleWorks, these programs are available in both the Windows and Mac environments; BibleWorks is PC only (though there are work-arounds to allow it to run on a Mac). Logos has the widest variety of secondary resources among the three, while BibleWorks and Accordance both pride themselves on making work with the Biblical text the center of focus.

In my experience, BibleWorks has a bit of a steeper learning curve than Accordance, but experienced, advanced users may find it to be fast and powerful. I personally have been a satisfied user of Accordance for about twenty years. The bottom line, though, is that all three are capable of helping with your Greek learning in the ways described below.

The "Big Three" computer software programs can give you instant parsing details (include lexical form and a gloss) for Greek words by hovering the cursor over the word you want to search. This is a great help in many circumstances, but you must be careful if you want to progress in your ability to read Greek! It becomes very easy just to hover the cursor over each word in the sentence. You may end up reading the glosses rather than reading the Greek (this, by the way, is the problem with using the old, print-based resources known as interlinear texts).

Another potential problem comes when you hover over words that you should have known. Rather than reinforcing the

---

1. As *Reboot Your Greek* was going to press, BibleWorks announced that it would "cease operation as a provider of Bible software tools" after twenty-six years.

mental pathways to the correct word forms in Greek, you shortcut the process and lose out on the opportunity to sharpen your Greek perception. The antidote to these problems is to hover your cursor as a method of last resort. Give yourself time to think about the difficult word before automatically moving the cursor.

I would also urge you to become familiar with the primary language grammatical tools built into your software. For example, search for all the nouns in Colossians 3 that are in the dative case. Search for all the infinitive verbs in Hebrews 6. After searching, compare the words that are found. What do they have in common? How are they different from other word forms? How are they different from one another? By studying in this way, you can reinforce and extend your familiarity with Greek morphology.

Lastly, I would suggest that you explore the syntax features of your software program (these often cost extra). See how the program developers have laid out the syntax of your favorite verses. Note the relationship between parsing and syntax (for example, the range of syntactical functions genitive nouns play). This is an opportunity to learn through exploration. See what exciting discoveries await you!

Exercise 39

1. Reread Ephesians 2:1–11. Look up at least one of the words you had marked for word study using blueletterbible.org.
2. If you don't already own Accordance, BibleWorks, or Logos Bible Software, download the trial version of one of them now. Be sure to get a Greek NT sampler along with the software. Read as many verses from the sampler as time allows. Use the instant details feature to help you with words you don't recognize right away.

Day 40: Review

Today ends your forty-day refresher. Take thirty seconds now to skim through each of the thirty-nine days prior to today. Remember the days that seemed easy—and the ones that seemed hard. Do they still seem hard, or have they gotten easier as you've remembered more of your Greek?

Focus on the topics of the last few days. Days 36 and 37 rounded out the coverage of participles with genitive absolutes (day 36) and periphrastic construction (day 37). Genitive absolutes are pretty straightforward, once you can get into the habit of suspecting one whenever you see a genitive participle. Remember that genitive absolutes have a genitive noun (or pronoun) as the "subject" of the genitive participle. Otherwise, they function pretty much like the adverbial participles we saw last week. Periphrastic construction is perhaps the easiest of all Greek participle usage—simply because they function almost exactly the same way as English verbs, namely, a *to be* verb plus a participle for certain tenses (such as I *am going*).

On days 38 and 39, we looked at various tools to help you maintain your progress in reading and understanding the Greek New Testament. Day 38 highlighted lexica (BDAG and Louw and Nida) and parsing guides (Han and Zerwick) you may wish to consult as aids to deeper understanding Greek words and word forms. On day 39 we looked at Bible software, which can provide many of the functions of the lexica and parsing guides, as well as offering many additional features to enrich your study.

Before I turn you over to the last exercise of the forty-day refresher, let me remind you of a couple of options for additional study. I already alluded to intermediate and advanced grammars back on day 20. Daniel B. Wallace's *Greek Grammar Beyond the*

Basics would be a good place to start if you want to dig deeper into the complexities of Koine Greek. Another option would be to do some reading of extrabiblical Koine Greek. A great resource for that is Rodney A. Whitacre's *A Patristic Greek Reader*. Like the *Reader's Edition Greek New Testament*, Whitacre's *Reader* offers translation helps in the footnotes to make your reading a joy.

Exercise 40

Look back at the exercises from the first few days of this forty-day journey one more time. See how much more readily you can read some of those verses now.

Remember the excitement and trepidation you felt on day 1. Take time to rejoice in how much progress you've made in your understanding and enjoyment of reading the Greek New Testament. Think about what commitments you want to make toward maintaining your ability to read Greek going into the future.

Day 41: Your Turn

Congratulations! You have completed your forty-day journey to reboot your Greek! I trust that you have enjoyed the journey, and that you are now much more confident in your ability to pick up your Greek New Testament and make your way through a reading.

I promised you a forty-day journey, so you may be wondering why there is a day 41 lesson. Good question! It's here to remind you that the most important day of the whole sequence is day 41. Today is the day in which you have to make a decision: will you continue to read Greek every day? The decision is yours. I've placed the resources and tools in your hand, but it's up to you to use them.

What will you read today?

Glossary

Accusative—one of the Greek noun cases; used primarily to indicate that the noun is being used as the direct object of a verb.

Antecedent—the noun that a pronoun takes the place of; the person, place, or thing to which the pronoun refers.

Aorist—one of the verb tenses. The aorist tense primarily indicates action of unspecified or unspecific duration. In the indicative mood, the aorist tense usually indicates that the action of the verb happened at a time before the sentence is uttered.

Apparatus—the text-critical notes at the bottom of the pages of a Greek New Testament.

Article—a word used to make a noun more definite; "the." (Unlike English, Greek has only a definite article.)

Aspect—the kind of action implied by a verb tense, especially ongoing versus simple action.

Augment—a morpheme used in Greek verbs to indicate past time; usually an epsilon added to the beginning of the verb stem.

Case—forms of Greek nouns used to indicate the noun's function in a sentence. The Greek cases are nominative, genitive, dative, accusative, and vocative.

Chunk—to break something down into smaller units (i.e., chunks), so that each chunk becomes more manageable.

Clause—a sentence or part of a sentence that contains at least a subject and a verb.

GLOSSARY

Dative—one of the Greek noun cases; used primarily to indicate that the noun is being used as the direct object of a verb. Also used frequently to indicate location (locative use) or item used to accomplish the action of the verb (instrumental use).

Declension—a distinct pattern by which nouns convey case. Greek has three declensions, called first, second, and third declensions.

Future—one of the verb tenses. In Greek, the future tense indicates action to take place at a time after the sentence is uttered.

Genitive—one of the Greek noun cases; used primarily to indicate that the noun is being used as a possessive. Usually translated with the helping word *of*.

Gloss—a one-word (or sometimes two- or three-word) substitute for a word in another language.

Imperative—one of the verb moods; used to express commands or requests.

Imperfect—one of the verb tenses. In Greek, the imperfect tense indicates ongoing action occurring prior to the time the sentence is uttered.

Indirect object—the recipient of the object of a verb.

Indicative—one of the verb moods; makes statements or asks questions about the way things were, are, will be, etc.

Infinitive—a verbal noun; one of the verb moods. In English, infinitives are formed by adding the word *to* to the simplest form of the verb.

Lexicon—a book that provides information about the meaning of words in another language. For our purposes, lexica (plural of lexicon) provide information in English about the meaning of Greek words.

GLOSSARY

Mood—the relation to reality expressed by the form of the verb. See indicative, subjunctive, optative, imperative, infinitive, participle.

Morpheme—the smallest part of a word that carries meaning.

Morphology—the study of the various forms Greek words take to convey their function in a sentence.

Nominative—one of the Greek noun cases; used primarily to indicate that the noun is being used as the subject of its sentence.

Noun—a word that represents a person, place, thing, etc.

Number—singular or plural; used for words in the noun system (nouns, pronouns, adjectives) and in the verb system.

Object—the recipient of the action of a verb.

Optative—one of the verb moods; rare in New Testament Greek. Similar to the subjunctive, but farther removed from the way things actually are.

Parse—to give the basic information encoded in the morphology of a specific word. For nouns, one parses by specifying the word's gender, number, case, and lexical form. For indicative verbs, full parsing requires specification of the word's person, number, tense, voice, mood, and lexical form.

Participle—a verbal adjective; one of the verb moods. In English, active participles are formed by adding -ing to the end of the verb, while passive participles are formed by adding -ed.

Perfect—one of the verb tenses. In Greek, the perfect tense indicates an action that took place prior to the time the sentence is uttered and whose ramifications are still being felt at the time of utterance.

Person—part of the parsing of verbs. Indicates whether the subject of the verb includes the speaker (1st person), the addressee (2nd person), or someone or something else (3rd person).

GLOSSARY

Pluperfect—one of the verb tenses. In Greek, the pluperfect tense indicates an action that took place prior to the past time event(s) described in the sentence and whose ramifications were still being felt at the time of those past event(s).

Preposition—a word that connects a noun or pronoun (the object of the preposition) to other parts of a sentence by expressing the relationship between the object and the other parts. Examples of prepositions in English include in, on, and through. Some common Greek prepositions are διά, ἐπί, and εἰς.

Present—one of the verb tenses. In Greek, the present tense primarily indicates ongoing action (though simple action is also possible). In the indicative mood, the present tense usually indicates that the action of the verb is happening at the time the sentence is uttered.

Principle parts—a list of six key first person singular indicative forms of a given verb in the order of Present Active, Future Active, Aorist Active, Perfect Active, Perfect Middle/Passive, and Aorist Passive. The principle parts of λύω are λύω, λύσω, ἔλυσα, λέλυκα, λέλυμαι, and ἐλύθην. All other forms of a Greek verb can be formed from these six "parts."

Pronoun—a word that takes the place of a noun.

Reduplication—the repetition of the first consonant of a verb, connected to the rest of the verb with an epsilon; used to indicate that the verb is in the perfect tense.

Slot—a place in a sentence where the sentence structure anticipates a particular kind of word, such as a noun, an adjective, or a verb.

Subject—the doer of the action of a verb (or the recipient of the action for a passive verb).

Subjunctive—one of the verb moods; used to indicate contingency, such as the way that things could, should, or might be.

GLOSSARY

Tense—the type of action or time-orientation expressed by a verb form. The Greek verb tenses are present, future, aorist, imperfect, perfect, and pluperfect.

Textual variant—a word or phrase where manuscripts of the Greek New Testament are not identical.

Verb—a word that communicates the action or state in a sentence.

Voice—the relationship between the subject and the verb as encoded in the verb form. The voices of the Greek verb are active (the subject does the action of the verb), middle (the subject is emphasized or does the action for himself/herself/itself/themselves), and passive (the subject receives the action of the verb).

Appendix A: Quick Start Guide (Nouns)

NOMINATIVE		N1. ὁ	N2. ἡ	N3. τό
ἐγώ	I	ἄνθρωπος	καρδία	τέκνον
σύ	you	person, a person	heart, a heart	child, a child
αὐτός	he	ὁ ἄνθρωπος	ἡ καρδία	τὸ τέκνον
αὐτή	she	the person	the heart	the child
αὐτό	it	ὁ ἀγαθὸς ἄνθρωπος	ἡ ἀγαθὴ καρδία	τὸ ἀγαθὸν τέκνον
ἡμεῖς	we	the good person	the good heart	the good child
ὑμεῖς	you	ὁ ἀνήρ	ἡ ζωή	τὸ πνεῦμα
αὐτοί	they	the man	the life	the Spirit
αὐταί	they	ὁ ἀγαθὸς ἀνήρ	ἡ ἀγαθὴ ζωή	τὸ ἀγαθὸν πνεῦμα
αὐτά	they	the good man	the good life	the good Spirit
GENITIVE		**G1. τοῦ**	**G2. τῆς**	**G3. τοῦ**
μου	my	ἀνθρώπου	καρδίας	τέκνου
σοῦ	your	of a person	of a heart	of a child
αὐτοῦ	his	τοῦ ἀνθρώπου	τῆς καρδίας	τοῦ τέκνου
αὐτῆς	her	of the person	of the heart	of the child
αὐτοῦ	its	τοῦ ἀγαθοῦ ἀνθρώπου	τῆς ἀγαθῆς καρδίας	τοῦ ἀγαθοῦ τέκνου
ἡμῶν	our	of the good person	of the good heart	of the good child
ὑμῶν	your	τοῦ ἀνδρός	τῆς ζωῆς	τοῦ πνεύματος
αὐτῶν	their	of the man	of the life	of the Spirit
αὐτῶν	their	τοῦ ἀγαθοῦ ἀνδρός	τῆς ἀγαθῆς ζωῆς	τοῦ ἀγαθοῦ πνεύματος
αὐτῶν	their	of the good man	of the good life	of the good Spirit
DATIVE		**D1. τῷ**	**D2. τῇ**	**D3. τῷ**
μοι	to me	ἀνθρώπῳ	καρδίᾳ	τέκνῳ
σοί	to you	to a person	to a heart	to a child
αὐτῷ	to him	τῷ ἀνθρώπῳ	τῇ καρδίᾳ	τῷ τέκνῳ
αὐτῇ	to her	to the person	to the heart	to the child
αὐτῷ	to it	τῷ ἀγαθῷ ἀνθρώπῳ	τῇ ἀγαθῇ καρδίᾳ	τῷ ἀγαθῷ τέκνῳ
ἡμῖν	to us	to the good person	to the good heart	to the good child
ὑμῖν	to you	τῷ ἀνδρί	τῇ ζωῇ	τῷ πνεύματι
αὐτοῖς	to them	to the man	to the life	to the Spirit
αὐταῖς	to them	τῷ ἀγαθῷ ἀνδρί	τῇ ἀγαθῇ ζωῇ	τῷ ἀγαθῷ πνεύματι
αὐτοῖς	to them	to the good man	to the good life	to the good Spirit
ACCUSATIVE		**A1. τόν**	**A2. τήν**	**A3. τό**
με	me	ἄνθρωπον	καρδίαν	τέκνον
σέ	you	person, a person	heart, a heart	child, a child
αὐτόν	him	τὸν ἄνθρωπον	τὴν καρδίαν	τὸ τέκνον
αὐτήν	her	the person	the heart	the child
αὐτό	it	τὸν ἀγαθὸν ἄνθρωπον	τὴν ἀγαθὴν καρδίαν	τὸ ἀγαθὸν τέκνον
ἡμᾶς	us	the good person	the good heart	the good child
ὑμᾶς	you	τὸν ἄνδρα	τὴν ζωήν	τὸ πνεῦμα
αὐτούς	them	the man	the life	the Spirit
αὐτάς	them	τὸν ἀγαθὸν ἄνδρα	τὴν ἀγαθὴν ζωήν	τὸ ἀγαθὸν πνεῦμα
αὐτά	them	the good man	the good life	the good Spirit

N4. οἱ	N5. αἱ	N6. τά
ἄνθρωποι	καρδίαι	τέκνα
people	hearts	children
οἱ ἄνθρωποι	αἱ καρδίαι	τὰ τέκνα
the people	the hearts	the children
οἱ ἀγαθοὶ ἄνθρωποι	αἱ ἀγαθαὶ καρδίαι	τὰ ἀγαθὰ τέκνα
the good people	the good hearts	the good children
οἱ ἄνδρες		τὰ πνεύματα
the men		the spirits
οἱ ἀγαθοὶ ἄνδρες		τὰ ἀγαθὰ πνεύματα
the good men		the good spirits

G4. τῶν	G5. τῶν	G6. τῶν
ἀνθρώπων	καρδιῶν	τέκνων
of people	of hearts	of children
τῶν ἀνθρώπων	τῶν καρδιῶν	τῶν τέκνων
of the people	of the hearts	of the children
τῶν ἀγαθῶν ἀνθρώπων	τῶν ἀγαθῶν καρδιῶν	τῶν ἀγαθῶν τέκνων
of the good people	of the good hearts	of the good children
τῶν ἀνδρῶν		τῶν πνευμάτων
of the men		of the spirits
τῶν ἀγαθῶν ἀνδρῶν		τῶν ἀγαθῶν πνευμάτων
of the good men		of the good spirits

D4. τοῖς	D5. ταῖς	D6. τοῖς
ἀνθρώποις	καρδίαις	τέκνοις
to people	to hearts	to children
τοῖς ἀνθρώποις	ταῖς καρδίαις	τοῖς τέκνοις
to the people	to the hearts	to the children
τοῖς ἀγαθοῖς ἀνθρώποις	ταῖς ἀγαθαῖς καρδίαις	τοῖς ἀγαθοῖς τέκνοις
to the good people	to the good hearts	to the good children
τοῖς ἀνδράσι(ν)		τοῖς πνεύμασι(ν)
to the men		to the spirits
τοῖς ἀγαθοῖς ἀνδράσι(ν)		τοῖς ἀγαθοῖς πνεύμασι(ν)
to the good men		to the good spirits

A4. τούς	A5. τάς	A6. τά
ἀνθρώπους	καρδίας	τέκνα
people	hearts	children
τοὺς ἀνθρώπους	τὰς καρδίας	τὰ τέκνα
the people	the hearts	the children
τοὺς ἀγαθοὺς ἀνθρώπους	τὰς ἀγαθὰς καρδίας	τὰ ἀγαθὰ τέκνα
the good people	the good hearts	the good children
τούς ἄνδρας		τὰ πνεύματα
the men		the spirits
τοὺς ἀγαθοὺς ἄνδρας		τὰ ἀγαθὰ πνεύματα
the good men		the good spirits

Appendix B: λύω Paradigm[1]

Principle Parts	λύω				λύσω	
	Pres. Act.	Imp. Act.	Pres. M/P	Imp. M/P	Fut. Act.	Fut. Mid.
Indic. S. 1.	λύω	ἔλυον	λύομαι	ἐλυόμην	λύσω	λύσομαι
2.	λύεις	ἔλυες	λύῃ	ἐλύου	λύσεις	λύσῃ
3.	λύει	ἔλυε(ν)	λύεται	ἐλύετο	λύσει	λύσεται
Pl. 1.	λύομεν	ἐλύομεν	λυόμεθα	ἐλυόμεθα	λύσομεν	λυσόμεθα
2.	λύετε	ἐλύετε	λύεσθε	ἐλύεσθε	λύσετε	λύσεσθε
3.	λύουσι(ν)	ἔλυον	λύονται	ἐλύοντο	λύσουσι(ν)	λύσονται
Subj. S. 1.	λύω		λύωμαι			
2.	λύσῃς		λύῃ			
3.	λύῃ		λύηται			
Pl. 1.	λύωμεν		λυώμεθα			
2.	λύητε		λύησθε			
3.	λύωσι(ν)		λύωνται			
Imper. S. 2.	λῦε		λύου			
3.	λυέτω		λυέσθω			
Pl. 2.	λύετε		λύεσθε			
3.	λυέτωσαν		λυέσθωσαν			
Infin.	λύειν		λύεσθαι			
Part.	λύων		λυόμενος			

1. Adapted from J. Gresham Machen, *New Testament Greek for Beginners* (Toronto: Macmillan, 1923), ¶ 589.

ἔλυσα		λέλυκα		λέλυμαι		ἐλύθην	
Aor. Act.	Aor. Mid.	Perf. Act.	Plup. Act.	Perf. M/P	Aor. Pass.		Fut. Pass.
ἔλυσα	ἐλυσάμην	λέλυκα	(ἐ)λελύκειν	λέλυμαι	ἐλύθην		λυθήσομαι
ἔλυσας	ἐλύσω	λέλυκας	(ἐ)λελύκεις	λέλυσαι	ἐλύθης		λυθήσῃ
ἔλυσε(ν)	ἐλύσατο	λέλυκε(ν)	(ἐ)λελύκει	λέλυται	ἐλύθη		λυθήσεται
ἐλύσαμεν	ἐλυσάμεθα	λελύκαμεν	(ἐ)λελύκειμεν	λελύμεθα	ἐλύθημεν		λυθησόμεθα
ἐλύσατε	ἐλύσασθε	λελύκατε	(ἐ)λελύκειτε	λέλυσθε	ἐλύθητε		λυθήσεσθε
ἔλυσαν	ἐλύσαντο	λελύκασι(ν) λέλυκαν	(ἐ)λελύκεισαν	λέλυνται	ἐλύθησαν		λυθήσονται
λύσω	λύσωμαι				λυθῶ		
λύσῃς	λύσῃ				λυθῇς		
λύσῃ	λύσηται				λυθῇ		
λύσωμεν	λυσώμεθα				λυθῶμεν		
λύσητε	λύσησθε				λυθῆτε		
λύσωσι(ν)	λύσωνται				λυθῶσι(ν)		
λῦσον	λῦσαι				λύθητι		
λυσάτω	λυσάσθω				λυθήτω		
λύσατε	λύσασθε				λύθητε		
λυσάτωσαν	λυσάσθωσαν				λυθήτωσαν		
λῦσαι	λύσασθαι	λελυκέναι		λελύσθαι	λυθῆναι		
λύσας	λυσάμενος	λελυκώς		λελυμένος	λυθείς		

Appendix C: Participle Paradigm

Present

Active, "loosing"

Sing.	N.	λύων	λύουσα	λῦον
	G.	λύοντος	λυούσης	λύοντος
	D.	λύοντι	λυούσῃ	λύοντι
	A.	λύοντα	λύουσαν	λῦον
Plur.	N.	λύοντες	λύουσαι	λύοντα
	G.	λυόντων	λυουσῶν	λυόντων
	D.	λύουσι(ν)	λυούσαις	λύουσι(ν)
	A.	λύοντας	λυούσας	λύοντα

Middle/Passive, "loosing (for oneself)/being loosed"

Sing.	N.	λυόμενος	λυομένη	λυόμενον
	G.	λυομένου	λυομένης	λυομένου
	D.	λυομένῳ	λυομένῃ	λυομένῳ
	A.	λυόμενον	λυομένην	λυόμενον
Plur.	N.	λυόμενοι	λυόμεναι	λυόμενα
	G.	λυομένων	λυομένων	λυομένων
	D.	λυομένοις	λυομέναις	λυομένοις
	A.	λυομένους	λυομένας	λυόμενα

	Masculine	Feminine	Neuter

Aorist
Active, "having loosed"

λύσας	λύσασα	λῦσαν
λύσαντος	λυσάσης	λύσαντος
λύσαντι	λυσάσῃ	λύσαντι
λύσαντα	λύσασαν	λῦσαν
λύσαντες	λύσασαι	λύσαντα
λυσάντων	λυσασῶν	λυσάντων
λύσασι(ν)	λυσάσαις	λύσασι(ν)
λύσαντας	λυσάσας	λύσαντα

Middle, "having loosed (for oneself)"

λυσάμενος	λυσαμένη	λυσάμενον
λυσαμένου	λυσαμένης	λυσαμένου
λυσαμένῳ	λυσαμένῃ	λυσαμένῳ
λυσάμενον	λυσαμένην	λυσάμενον
λυσάμενοι	λυσάμεναι	λυσάμενα
λυσαμένων	λυσαμένων	λυσαμένων
λυσαμένοις	λυσαμέναις	λυσαμένοις
λυσαμένους	λυσαμένας	λυσάμενα

Passive, "having been loosed"

λυθείς	λυθεῖσα	λυθέν
λυθέντος	λυθείσης	λυθέντος
λυθέντι	λυθείσῃ	λυθέντι
λυθέντα	λυθεῖσαν	λυθέν
λυθέντες	λυθεῖσαι	λυθέντων
λυθέντων	λυθεισῶν	λυθέντων
λυθεῖσι(ν)	λυθείσαις	λυθεῖσι(ν)
λυθέντας	λυθείσας	λυθέντα

| Masculine | Feminine | Neuter |

Perfect
Active, "having loosed (with present results)"

λελυκώς	λελυκυῖα	λελυκός
λελυκότος	λελυκυίας	λελυκότος
λελυκότι	λελυκυίᾳ	λελυκότι
λελυκότα	λελυκυῖαν	λελυκός
λελυκότες	λελυκυῖαι	λελυκότα
λελυκότων	λελυκυιῶν	λελυκότων
λελυκόσι(ν)	λελυκυίαις	λελυκόσι(ν)
λελυκότας	λελυκυίας	λελυκότα

Middle/Passive, "loosed"

λελύμενος	λελυμένη	λελύμενον
λελυμένου	λελυμένης	λελυμένου
λελυμένῳ	λελυμένῃ	λελυμένῳ
λελύμενον	λελυμένην	λελύμενον
λελύμενοι	λελύμεναι	λελύμενα
λελυμένων	λελυμένων	λελυμένων
λελυμένοις	λελυμέναις	λελυμένοις
λελυμένους	λελυμένας	λελύμενα

| Masculine | Feminine | Neuter |

Appendix D: Participle Flowchart
Translating the Present Active Participle

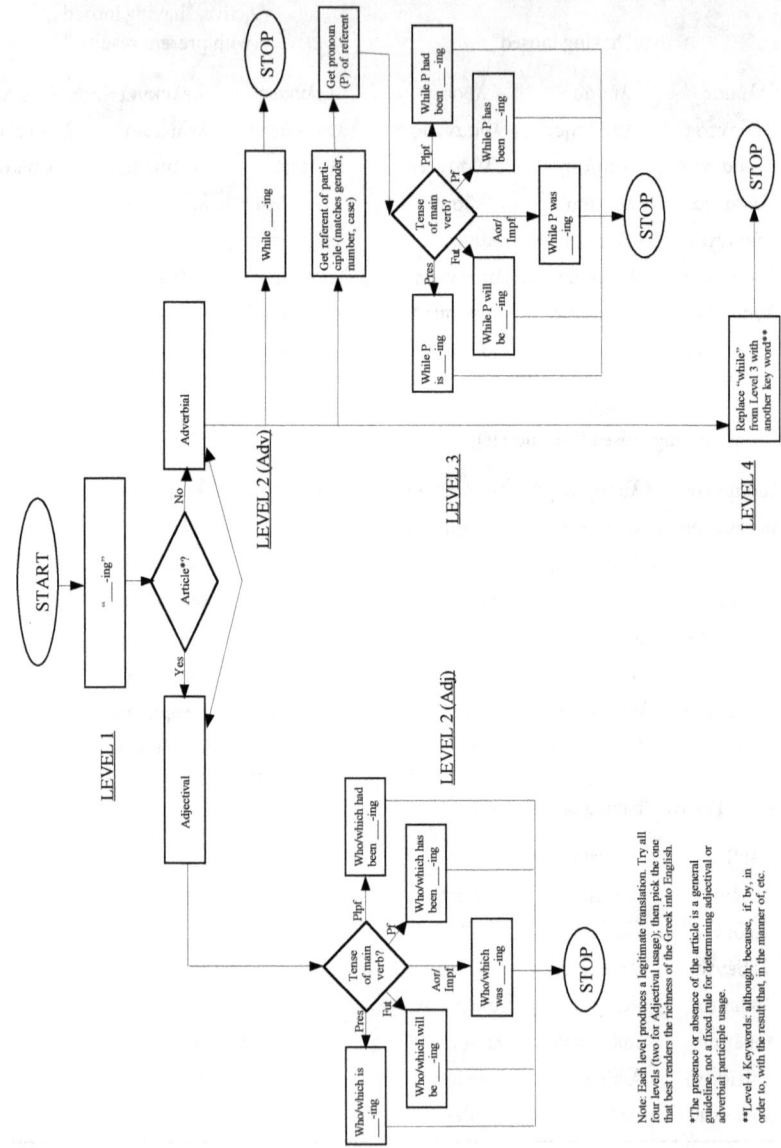

www.ingramcontent.com/pod-product-compliance
Lightning Source LLC
Chambersburg PA
CBHW072147160426
43197CB00012B/2286